Conquering

the

Culture

The Fight for Our Children's Souls

by David Paul Eich

HUNTINGTON HOUSE PUBLISHERS

Huntington House Publishers
P.O. Box 53788
Lafayette, Louisiana 70505

Library of Congress Card Catalog Number 95-77215
ISBN 1-56384-101-0

Printed in the U.S.A.

Dedication

— ❁ —————————————————————————

To Kathy Schleicher for the countless debates we had on style, grammar and logic. Fortunately, you won.

To Gale Podnar and Sheila McLouth for putting up with change after change. Never forget the "gift of change."

To Janet Chordas (a best friend to my best friend) who took the time to share her editing skills.

To Dr. Ray Guarendi, without whose encouragement for the project and confidence in a fellow Christian, this book would not have been.

And finally to the love of my life—my family.

To my Cindy and our children, Robbie, Andrew and Kelly, whom I am eternally proud of.

God Bless You All.

Long before the first words were put on paper for *Conquering the Culture: The Fight For Our Children's Souls*, I was determined to dedicate my work to the Holy Spirit. In that light, there is a wonderful Irish Christian singer by the name of Dana. Following are her words. May they ever remain in your heart.

> Come Holy Spirit, fill our hearts, enkindle in us, the
> fire of Your love.
>
> —Dana, from her Rosary tape

Contents

Chapter 3: Hell's Heroes

Chapter 4: To Face the Wind

Chapter 5: If I Only Had a Brain

Foreword

Only two possibilities contend for the ultimate truth: God created humans or humans created God. The truth of one fully precludes the truth of the other. If God made us, then He alone knows the absolute best way to live. He is the master parent, the master teacher, the master psychologist, the master sociologist. He designed the human race, so he knew perfectly how we ought to think and conduct ourselves.

If humans created God, then knowing the best way to live lies somewhere within our collective wisdom. We alone are able, indeed bound, as our species evolves, to discover more healthy and fulfilling ways to guide ourselves. The process of discarding pre-civilized spiritual myths of absolute right and wrong is necessary to move forward as a culture or race.

As Dr. James Dobson has put it, we are in the midst of a cultural war between those who believe God is and those who believe He isn't. This war is by no means unique to our time. It first appeared when man did what he did in the Garden of Eden. In the beginning, man wanted to be as God; to make his own rules and morals. And, so it has been ever since.

Through the ages, man's wisdom has often had the sound of truth, even as it has changed with time. God's wisdom has remained immutable. Man's wisdom is temporary, suited to his passing desires. God's wisdom is permanently designed for ultimate good. As the human race sees itself as more sophisticated, it sees itself as wiser. It no longer needs the ancient standards and truths. Those were for another time, a simpler society.

In *Conquering the Culture: The Fight for Our Children's Souls*, David Paul Eich has captured the essence of modern man striving to be his own god. To the casual thinker, the words and meaning of Darcee make sense. They present a new and improved way to live. They are the dominant philosophy of our time.

A defining characteristic of our culture is the desire for what sounds good, what will, as St. Paul says, "tickle our ears." Only through scrutiny do Darcee's ways ring hollow, as does the treachery that has enveloped humankind since the beginning.

Danika, personifying the Christian world view, tells parents there are indeed certain right ways to think and live. These are not only morally right but psychologically and culturally sound. Danika says that man doesn't make the best rules; God does.

Conquering the Culture: The Fight for Our Children's Souls is a debate for the hearts and minds of our children. Listen closely for which side makes the most sense. There you'll find "truth."

—Dr. Raymond Guarendi
Clinical Psychologist & Author

Prologue

Although the dialogue that comprises this book is fictional, the topics covered are all too real. Most readers will find themselves identifying with the correspondents who seek—or give—advice after the positions described in the following advertisement are filled.

PARENTAL CONSULTANTS WANTED for a unique assignment helping parents raise children. Our group represents an amalgamation of the American spirit with traditional and single parents, and blended families. We seek the counsel of qualified experts for guidance on the following:

Morals & Values: Is there a difference? How and what do we teach children? Why?

Love & Discipline: Can the two go together? Where do we (or should we) draw the line?

Rights & Responsibilities: What is the real "parenting" difference? What about children's rights? What can/must we expect?

Societal Pressures: How do we handle issues like sexual expression, cultural diversity, materialism, drugs and violence, religious freedom, respect for life, environmental stewardship, freedom of speech, hero worship, social justice and entertainment industry images and messages?

Educational Ethics: What positions should we take on condom distribution, sex education, school prayer, value-neutral instruction, and parental involvement?

With children's best interests in mind, consultants will be chosen to provide expertise in the aforementioned areas. Those selected will be capable of balancing historical and factual data with common sense and fairness.

Recognizing the diversity of opinions on how to raise children, our parents reserve the right to select two or more consultants whose counsel may represent conflicting positions. This will ensure that interested parties have the opportunity to review, critique, and provide opposing arguments that are critical to raising happy, healthy, responsible adults. Views will be expressed in writing to prevent misinterpretation and misrepresentation. Correspondence should be thorough, honest, and creative.

If you feel you are qualified to handle this assignment, please send your resume and cover letter to:

Parent's Group
5683 First Street
Mir, Montana 53787

Attention: Paul, Town Elder

---

26 December

Dear Parent Group Representatives:

Congratulations! As you know, the Mir, Montana Parent's Association has elected you to represent our community in conversations with two parenting consultants. These professionals have been contracted to provide expert advice in the art and science of raising children.

Danika will represent a more traditional approach to childrearing, whereas, Darcee will speak from a "modernist" point-of-view.

Correspondence should be mailed to each consultant with a copy to me. Danika and Darcee will respond in writing to your questions.

Following completion of each topical area (morals and values, love and discipline, rights and responsibilities, societal pressures and educational ethics) I will summarize all positions with a series of probing questions designed to stimulate discussion among parents in your organization.

You may begin your correspondence the first of the year. Good luck and may God give you the wisdom to discern how best to protect the children and families of Mir, Montana.

Paul, Town Elder

---

26 December

Dear Danika and Darcee:

Congratulations! You have been selected to provide consulting advice to the Parents' Association of Mir, Montana. We feel fortunate that our group was able to engage the services of two highly respected consultants whose parental philosophies will most assuredly enhance the parenting skills of our members.

Danika, you will be happy to know that Darcee represents the highest standards of professionalism, with positions on community boards and university faculty. We can expect recommendations to follow the latest research in the science of raising children.

Darcee, you too will be pleased as Danika will offer "homespun" advice based on traditional positions commonly found outside academic circles.

Each of you will receive the first of several letters from representatives of our parents' group. Your responses to their questions will be shared to allow each consultant to add to, agree with, or challenge the other's position.

Allow me to introduce those parents who will test both your intellect and common sense.

Brina, a stay-at-home mom and her husband Hasheem, will represent the traditional family with four children ages six through fourteen.

Ronica and John are younger parents working full time to raise three children ages two, five, and six.

Gillie is a single dad whose wife passed away just after their second baby was born. He is now raising two children ages seven and four.

Vasya is also a single parent raising three children ages five, seven, and nine. She was divorced after ten years of marriage.

Last, but certainly not least, are Janet and Richard. These two fine individuals will raise issues from a grandparent's perspective. They have five grandchildren ages one through fifteen.

These parents and grandparents will address five key themes. First, values. Or, if you prefer, morals, and what has happened to these time-honored beacons. Second, freedoms and their implications. Third, heroes. Who are they now? And why? Fourth, justice and the subject of fairness. Finally, education, with all its ethical dilemmas.

Be honest, be frank, and remember, it is because we love our children that we seek your counsel.

Paul, Town Elder

Chapter One

In Search of Morals

Values are the emotional rules by which a nation governs itself. Values summarize the accumulated folk wisdom by which a society organizes and disciplines itself. And values are the previous reminders that individuals obey to bring order and meaning into their personal lives. Without values, nations, societies and individuals can pitch straight to hell.

—James Michener

Part I
Wandering in the Moral Desert

Morality was made for man, not man for morality.
—Israel Rangwill
Children of the Ghetto

---

1 January

Dear Darcee and Danika:

We're the old folks Paul spoke about. We have three children, all married, and five grandchildren. It is the latter we are most concerned about.

In our parenting days we had less to worry about than we do as grandparents today. Forty years ago parents were concerned about polio, communism, and the bomb. Schools were safe, drugs were unheard of, and "aides" were found in hospitals, assisting nurses.

When we raised our children, mom stayed at home until they were in high school. Our kids understood the consequences of bad manners. They understood that TV time was a privilege. They knew Sundays were reserved for God, and the Ten Commandments were not, as Ted Koppel stated, suggestions. Children were taught to love the flag and to respect the beliefs of our forefathers.

Our children's heroes, like kids' heroes today, often came from the entertainment industry. Back then, baseball stars played for the love of the game; movie stars won academy awards for playing positive role models—not sadistic killers who cannibalized their victims. And TV families were made up of real families, not single parents whose morals would have been condemned.

There was no talk of values. Telling right from wrong was easy. Teenage sex, and, for that matter, sex outside marriage was wrong! Teen pregnancy was shameful, not a status symbol. Discipline was the rule—no questions asked. If kids were spoiled it was with love, not designer clothes, electronic gadgetry, or freedom from the watchful eyes of caring parents.

As grandparents we see too many children struggling to overcome peer pressure, fostered by a school system that has abdicated responsibility; a Hollywood that has abandoned good taste; a government whose retreat from God is camouflaged behind the First Amendment; and parents whose "me generation" mentality has sown the seeds for an even more selfish, hedonistic, and violent society.

Is there hope? Are we seeing ghosts? Is this just a phase in which we should say "this too shall pass"? If not, please tell us what we and grandparents everywhere can do to save the children.

Jan and Richard

5 January

Dear Jan & Richard:

Though many of your concerns are commonplace among today's grandparents, let me reassure both of you that children and families of the nineties have before them wonderful opportunities to make this world a better place.

You mentioned that the fifties were easier times with only health and international obstacles standing in the way of a stress-free world. During this same decade racism was rampant throughout America. Alcoholism was at epidemic proportions—especially among working fathers. And, speaking of fathers, long hours and a "children-should-be-seen-and-not-heard" mentality often led to physical and emotional abuse.

Moms were confined in the home, left to find meaning in laundry tubs, kitchen stoves and dusty furniture. That's one reason why the divorce rate began escalating in the fifties. Fortunately, as the decade ended, so did the stigma of "staying together for the children."

Other points to remember are that the fifties and every generation before and after experienced teen pregnancy, drug abuse, discipline problems, and a host of other obstacles. This was also the decade where parental religious zeal often led children to question the very existence of God.

On the positive side, your parenting generation began to experience the tremendous education and communication potential of television. Progress was made in classifying multiple disorders associated with broken families or parental abuse. First Amendment freedoms began to flourish as the children of the fifties became adults. Today many of your generation's offspring are responsible for the growth of children's rights, cultural diversity, and the rising influence of women.

Thanks to your children we have a country where each individual, regardless of sex, age, or upbringing, can pursue happiness free of puritanical and fundamentalist perversions.

Your grandchildren will not be subject to other's morality. They will have the option to choose their own Eastern, Western, or New-Age philosophies. Their lifestyles will benefit from technologies conducive to personal growth and freedom. Their potential for happiness will exceed all previous generations as they maximize their capacity to develop from within.

Will there be challenges? Absolutely. But remember— crime, violence, sexually transmitted diseases—like the poor, will always be with us. Just as your grandparents could not understand your music, dress, and idols, so too will you find it difficult to accept the styles and tastes of your grandchildren. Today's Madonna was yesterday's Elvis, today's marijuana was yesterday's cigarettes, and today's "time out" was yesterday's "grounded." Nothing really changes—only the labels.

As you hinted, this is just a phase that, like its predecessors, will pass. And, as it does, your grandchildren will experience progress and independence unheard of in your time.

So relax, sit back, and don't worry about the children. Just as you matured, so will the kids. Remember, the number one threat to this nation is "experts" who continue to paint a negative picture, ultimately leading to the destruction of the modern family. Don't let that happen.

Darcee

---

5 January

Dear Jan & Richard:

You have both stated a number of issues which demand a thorough response on my part. First, I emphatically state: "No! You are not seeing ghosts!"

The problems you mention are not only real, but are escalating in intensity. There can be no quarrel that families in the nineties face unprecedented pressures which were unheard of only forty years before.

Perhaps the best indicator of change is Hollywood's portrayal of the American family. In the fifties, programs like "Father Knows Best," "Ozzie and Harriet," and the "Donna Reed Show" all depicted families consisting of strong parents and good kids. Children faced the same challenges kids face today—neighborhood squabbles, teachers who seemed to demand too much, parents who demanded more; first love, first date, first heartbreak.

The sixties introduced the "unconventional" with "The Addams' Family," the "Flintstones," and a trend for widowed fathers with programs like the "Andy Griffith Show," "My Three Sons," and "The Rifleman." Only "Leave It to Beaver" seemed to cling to the nuclear family persona.

In 1971 a new family emerged that set the stage for Hollywood's profile of the more "normal family." Archie Bunker and company brought atheism, racism, abortion, and homosexuality into family rooms across America. Meanwhile, "The Brady Bunch" introduced the "blended" family, while shows like "Alice" and "One Day At A Time" cornered the divorce market. Ironically, nuclear family scenarios were packaged as memorabilia with the likes of "Little House on the Prairie," the "Waltons," and "Happy Days."

The eighties Huxtables clearly clashed with the valueless "Married With Children." Other first-time arrangements began to appear with "Full House," TV's version of *Three Men and a Baby*. "Who's The Boss" depicted the first surrogate-man-housekeeper-father and almost live-in lover character. A bizarre situation indeed.

The nineties promise not only new family permutations but also a candid look at the very issues addressed in your letter.

Murphy Brown-type characters will continue to paint a positive single parent portfolio, Roseanne will be admired for the safe-sex strategies offered to her daughter, and The Simpsons will make a mockery of family, God, and country.

Given current cultural trends, the nineties will bring a host of media, entertainment, government, and educational experts whose anti-moral crusade will continue to weaken the one institution capable of loving children—the family. These characters will chastise those of us who dare to ignore their environmental warnings, tolerance for cultural diversity, anti-business campaign, freedom of choice initiatives, and First Amendment agendas. They will promote children's rights at the expense of parental responsibility, while their value-neutral lifestyles reach out to the children and parents who are most vulnerable to day-to-day pressures.

Moms will be taught that it's okay to work full time; that their children will survive and be stronger for it. Kids will continue to adore entertainment personalities whose inappropriate behavior represents the antithesis of strong family values. Teenagers will learn to demand new freedoms and new defenses when their rebellious lifestyles run amuck with unsympathetic authorities.

And, if this isn't enough, the only mention of God will likely come in yet another story about clergy who violate innocents.

Is there hope, you ask? Absolutely! Anytime citizens begin to question the direction a moral nation should pursue, there is hope. When we recognize the decline in manners, discipline, and self-control among our youth—there's hope. When we reach out on behalf of other parents for the sake of children—there's hope. And, most important, when we are willing to get involved to save a child, a family, and a nation—there's hope.

Your involvement began with this letter. Now you must continue your journey gathering and sharing information with other parents of Mir, Montana. As your group begins to sift through the advice from Darcee and me, your mission will become clear.

Danika

10 January

Dear Darcee and Danika:

Your comments generated some interesting discussion.

Danika, we found your TV family chronology interesting and wondered why so many experts are critical of the
fifties. These professionals typically belittle the fifties as an
era to which no intelligent parent would wish to return.
Frankly, we agree to a point. The idea of "returning to
yesteryear" is, at best, fiction.

Darcee, your enthusiasm for the future was both refreshing and unsettling. It was refreshing in the sense that
parents and grandparents tend to always hear the negative; unsettling, in that we feel you cannot ignore what
appears to be a continuing decline in the morals of our
children.

Please review your position and that of each other,
and comment accordingly.

Jan and Richard

15 January

Dear Jan and Richard:

Rest assured that I do not ignore the multiple pressures and problems our kids face today. But, as I alluded
to in my letter, progressive parents will produce independent thinkers whose maturation will only enhance the
planet.

The litany of problems exposed by Danika are real.
However, so too are the solutions. With education we can
expect more responsible behavior. For instance, the "Say
No To Drugs" campaign is making a favorable impact on
our youth. Kids whose self-esteem has been damaged are
now coming forward to teachers and other authorities.
Adolescents with access to sex education classes are better
prepared to handle this critical growing up stage. And,
today's teenagers are ready to defend the environment,

religion, and the First Amendment, while respecting the dignity of others.

These examples represent positive signs that parents are doing just fine, kids are progressing, and society as a whole is maturing. As grandparents, you can encourage your grandchildren to explore life with all its opportunities, by reminding their parents that kids must have the right to experience childhood freedoms. Children who are exposed to different cultures and lifestyles will learn tolerance. Finally, parental responsibility must never interfere with the child's quest for positive self-esteem.

Remember, morals are derived from values and values from parents. If parents teach tolerance, privacy, social justice, self-esteem, independence, and a genuine respect for the environment and Bill of Rights, their kids will live in a better world.

                                                Darcee

---

                                          15 January

Dear Jan & Richard:

When challenged with the argument that you should never return to the fifties, remember it was the era when sodomy was recognized as evil. In the fifties, children could safely walk down streets, go to the bookstore, library, or movie house—and not have to grow up too fast. It was a time when perversion, pornography, and pedophilia were not protected by First Amendment radicalism; when pregnancy rates for teens were down and graduation rates were up; when there was no AIDS and fewer STDs; and teenage crime, addicts, divorces, abortion, poverty, incarceration, and single parents were rare.

In the fifties, one might be surprised to find that bestsellers included *Betty Crocker's Cookbook*, the Holy Bible, and Art Linkletter's *Kids Say the Darndest Things*. Moving forward, sixties literature took a different twist with the *Human Sexual Response* and *The Death of a President*. The seventies brought a President's downfall (*The Final Days*) while in the privacy of our bedrooms we were sensitized to *The Sensuous Man* and *The Sensuous Woman*. In the eighties, we were told to get in shape with Jane Fonda and Wall Street as "Top 10" sellers focused on bodies and budgets.

Music followed similar patterns. Fifties music included songs like "A Bushel and a Peck" and the "Ballad of Davey Crockett." In the sixties, "flower children" and "the boys from Brit" stirred a nation of youth. The seventies' Bee-Gees told us that "Staying Alive" was the goal. Music messages of the eighties offered a different sort of workout with "Let's Get Physical." But, in the early nineties music titles took a back seat to group names like the B-52s, Seduction, Cover Girls, Bad English, Guns 'n' Roses, and 2-Live-Crew. Parents became horrified, and youth delighted, as messages of racism, suicide, violence, sexual exploitation, drug and alcohol abuse, and satanic worship crisscrossed the air waves.

Returning to the fifties, audiences applauded movies like *Ben Hur* and *From Here to Eternity*. Popular movies in the sixties included *West Side Story*, *The Sound of Music*, and *Midnight Cowboy*. (The latter was the first X-rated movie to win an Academy Award.) In the seventies, we were introduced to the physical violence of *The Godfather* and the emotional violence of *Kramer versus Kramer*. With the eighties, *Platoon* reminded us of the fifty-five thousand who died in Vietnam, while *E.T.* captured our hearts.

Leading *Time* magazine articles of the fifties captured the country's attention with stories about big-city crime and education. *Time* stories of the sixties questioned morals, maturity, and whether we could trust anyone over thirty. In the seventies, heroin hit home and crime gripped our forgotten children. With the eighties *Time* revealed that we, as a society, were beginning to question the value of television. Cover stories asked—"Who's teaching our children?"—while trying to figure out why there was so much violence in the home.

It's easy for Darcee to caution against those who trumpet danger. But, poverty affects one child in five; SAT scores are falling and dropout figures rising; growing numbers of young people can't fill out a job application; diseases such as whooping cough are again on the rise; and the AIDS epidemic is reaching children and teenagers across the country. Speaking of teens, girls as young as twelve get pregnant while boys as young as eight join gangs and are forced to carry "protection" to school.

The challenge is not to return to the '50s; the challenge is to return to morals.

Danika

PART II
"What Is Truth?"

I cannot believe that this country cannot come together around some values. What these kids need is a moral life. The issue is not ideas, it's conduct. The real question is how we reach these young people morally, and what do we bring to them?

—Robert Coles
Harvard Professor of Psychiatry

15 January

Dear Darcee and Danika:

We are both twenty-eight, raising three children ages two, five and six. Like other parents, we are confused over the continuous discussions about family values. Everywhere we turn it seems some politician or newscaster is trying to reach a consensus as to what values really mean.

Neither of us recalls this topic being of such importance when we were growing up. I guess our parents took for granted that values, like morals, were something handed down from generation to generation.

Are we naive? Complacent? Or simply out of touch? How and when should we address family values with our children? What values should we stress? And, will these values be accepted by other parents whose concern for raising children parallels our own?

Parents look to both of you to help us develop our moral compass.

John and Ronica

---

18 January

Dear John & Ronica:

The mere fact that you and other parents are troubled by "family values" suggests that something is wrong. When you hear others question the absence of morals among our youth, you realize that something must be done. And, when experts argue that you can't "legislate morality," you agree that this subject should not be discussed on the Senate floor, in the judge's chambers, or the oval office.

You are not naive, complacent, or out of touch. But, you are troubled. As you set standards you will learn who stands against you. Often, these individuals will come from your neighborhood, work, school, or family.

Confusing terms and phrases such as "value neutral," "situation ethics," "values clarification" and "relativity" surface, causing parents to contemplate Pilate's inquiry, "What is truth?" Take heart. Your conscience will provide a moral code and confirm that teaching moral values is necessary in developing a child's character.

Contrary to what others may say, your thoughts will eventually echo those of William Bennett (former Secretary of Education) who stated:

> We should not use the fact that there are many difficult and controversial moral questions as an argument against basic instruction in a subject. After all, we do not argue against teaching physics because laser physics is difficult, against teaching biology or chemistry because gene splicing and cloning are complex and controversial, against teaching American history because there are heated disputes about the founder's intent. Every field has its complexities and controversies. And every field has its basics, its fundamentals, so too with forming character and achieving moral literacy.

Do not fall for arguments which ask: Whose values? Yours or mine? By whose standards? Under what conditions? Using what logic? According to what law? By whose authority? Use common sense. Who can legitimately argue that teaching honesty, charity, or diligence, is harmful? Impress upon the opposition that there is nothing wrong with standing up for your beliefs, that being open-minded doesn't have to preclude personal convictions, and that morality is not an affront to others. Rather, it involves commitment to family, country, and God.

Develop your children's moral principles. Talk about family values, what they mean and why they're important. Remember, failure to instill values in today's children invites others to instill their values in tomorrow's adults.

Danika

---

18 January

Dear John & Ronica:

Your insightful questions demonstrate why there's so much confusion over family values and morals. The following comments may help demystify the subject.

You mentioned that a "family values" discussion never occurred in your home. Ironically, when your parents were your age, nightly newscasts were split between racism and Vietnam. A President, his brother, and a civil rights leader were assassinated. A later President rose to power only to be forced out of office. Your parents' generation profited from the greedy eighties while the number of children living in poverty nearly doubled.

Yet, this same generation has begun to yearn for the moral foundation that belonged to earlier times. A paradox indeed. Either our country had a strong moral code which was ignored, or morals really have little to do with history. Let me explain.

Those who hold that Judeo-Christian morals represent our constitutional road map conveniently forget that religion was often a scourge, driving people to seek the new land. In fact, intolerance for people of different cultures, ethnicity, and religious beliefs was often magnified by Judeo-Christian fanatics.

In addition, you will hear the argument that our nation's laws are a derivative of the Ten Commandments. That suggests pre-Mosaic civilizations tolerated random murder, stealing, and lying. However, we know that Egyptians, Phonecians, and Greeks had strict laws to deal with disorder.

Family values, like commandments, are guidelines. And your choices may not parallel the moral philosophies of other parents. Frankly, that's the good news. One standard of childraising you don't want to be caught up in, is passing judgment on those whose values are inconsistent with your own.

If your parental philosophy abhors physical discipline, then why should you be criticized by parents whose style may one day be questioned by authorities? If you choose to let your children experience different religious philosophies, why should you be questioned by rigid parents whose intolerance may drive their children away from God? If your moral code balances sex education with an adolescent's natural tendencies, why should you be questioned for protecting your child from pregnancy—or worse—AIDS? Why should you be ridiculed by others who believe their values, morals, and convictions will work for your family?

You have the right to judge what is best for you, just as your children will share what is best for them. Together, you will grow in respecting one another's needs. And one day, your children will give the gift of independence to your grandchildren—a gift that too many parents "manage" at the expense of their child's growth potential.

Refrain from judgmental family values discussions and you will avoid being judged by those whose opinions really count—your children.

Darcee

21 January

Dear Darcee and Danika:

Enclosed are copies of each other's initial commentary on family values. Please critique the opposing position and provide further rationale on why we should adopt your philosophy.

Recognize that as parents we believe it is our responsibility to give our children values. Subsequently, we request your assistance in the identification of those values.

John and Ronica

24 January

Dear John and Ronica:

Danika's point about "legislating morality" clearly adopts my position. Danika stated that the debate begins in the home. This is why values, like morals, are unique to each family's situation.

This logic brings me to my second point. Danika's inference that terms like "situation ethics" are contrary to some moral code is, at best, contradictory. Each situation demands a code of behavior. This position is a universal truth. Morals are defined by a kaleidoscope of character/ event interactions. As each new encounter unfolds, so will the appropriate behavior. We must teach our children that "relative" terms mean nothing more than selecting values which are right for them—values which develop character capable of applying the right moral mix to the right situation.

To assist you in your "family values" selection, consider the following:

- teaching children their right *to privacy.*
- teaching children to respect the *dignity of others* regardless of ethnic, culture, or lifestyle.
- teaching children *respect for authority* outside the home.

- teaching children *social justice* ensuring a fair distribution of wealth.
- teaching children *integrity* in selecting personal wants and needs.
- teaching children their *rights* under the law.
- teaching children *self-esteem*.
- teaching children *independence*.
- teaching children to protect the *environment* and *animals*.
- teaching children to tap their *spiritual* strength from within.
- teaching children *courage* to stand up for the oppressed.
- teaching children *loyalty* to the Bill of Rights and Constitution.
- teaching children *peace* through disarmament.

These values represent the foundation for raising responsible youth. But, you can't and shouldn't be expected to achieve this goal alone. Fortunately, assistance from a variety of experts will ensure that your children experience future success and acceptance in the universal family.

Darcee

---

24 January

Dear John and Ronica:

As I read Darcee's letter, I began to wonder what the world would be like if everyone designed one's own moral code. Imagine parents and children selecting values according to their needs.

Teens could justify promiscuity based on a need to reduce peer pressure. Adolescents could demand tasteless attire as a necessary self-esteem symbol. Youngsters could rationalize TV viewing habits as a principle of children's rights. And parents could abdicate parental responsibilities because of lifestyle changes.

Values are not laws any more than morals are com-

mandments. However, laws, like commandments, provide
do's and don'ts for a moral society. And, without parental
values children have little reason to obey, much less understand, the law.

If there is no standard of right or wrong, then one
group could condemn the actions of a child abuser while
another sees only the need for tolerance. Syndicated columnist, Don Feder asks, "What makes the morality of
those who hid Jews during the Holocaust superior to those
who killed them?"

Darcee's position appeals to human pride with her
"why should you" arguments. Here's why. If parents choose
not to discipline their children, others will. Teachers,
judges, and employers will have little trouble with
undisciplined youth. The question is not what type of discipline, the question is whether to discipline.

If parents choose to condescend to the sexual desires
of their children, they jeopardize not only their kids, but
their children's partners, who risk disease, pregnancy, and
possible death.

If parents allow their children to follow religious "pied
pipers," they may find themselves de-programming sons
and daughters who have become spiritually detached from
mom and dad.

It's better to have children question why there are
limits than to have them ask why their parents allowed
them to fail.

Responding to the second part of your letter, the following values will ensure morally courageous children.

- *Privacy* - Recognizing each person's right to personal property, attitudes, and beliefs.
- *Authority* - Acknowledging the legitimacy of rules
  and limits and the right of others, especially parents, to enforce them.
- *Temperance* - Exercising self-control in the management of resources and/or avoid excess in behavior and lifestyle.

- *Conviction* - Standing strong in one's beliefs.
- *Compassion* - Sensitivity toward those experiencing hardships.
- *Charity* - Possessing sympathetic disposition to help the needy and suffering.
- *Self-Discipline* - Controlling one's behavior, desires, and passions for the sake of personal welfare and/or the welfare of others.
- *Sense of Humor/Play* - Enjoying life with the ability to laugh at one's own humanness.
- *Honesty* - Respecting the truth and acting accordingly.
- *Humility* - Having an appropriate sense of reserve toward the recognition of one's own talents and blessings.
- *Thankfulness* - Possessing a full sense of awareness of how much God has given oneself, parents, and others.
- *Diligence* - Having a strong work ethic.
- *Citizenship* - Serving one's country.
- *Sanctity of Life* - Acknowledging that all human life is sacred, from conception to death.
- *Responsibility* - Learning to make decisions and accept the consequences.
- *Forbearance* - The ability to accept difficult circumstances.
- *Discernment* - Being able to make wise decisions guided by a sense of right and wrong.
- *Social Justice* - Desiring equal treatment of others, regardless of social standing.
- *Forgiveness* - Ceasing to feel resentment against another.

These values come from a spiritual foundation. Belief in God, while living according to His principles, is the spiritual glue which holds families together.

Danika

Part III
The Family . . . New and Improved?

Where does the family start? It starts with a young man falling in love with a girl. No superior alternative has yet been found.

—Sir Winston Churchill

All happy families resemble one another; every unhappy family is unhappy in its own way.

—Tolstoy

---

2 February

Dear Danika and Darcee:

Like Gillie, I'm a single parent. Unlike Gillie, who lost his spouse, I chose to divorce mine. My children, ages five, seven and nine are well-adjusted, accepting my mother/father role. We are a family. I say this with pride and confidence.

However, I'm concerned that my single-parent model is lost in some bureaucrat's definition, balanced between liberal or conservative leanings.

Please provide your perception as to what a family is, or should be, whether or not "traditional" is preferred and if so, why? And why is there so much "hullabaloo" over the word, meaning, and importance of family?

Vasya

---

5 February

Dear Vasya:

Your concern over the definition and importance of family has generated a great deal of discussion. Unfortunately, what was once a simple term capturing the essence of parenthood and childhood, has since become a convoluted human arrangement.

Before providing a definition of family, I will address

those issues which are responsible for all the fuss. Two words come to mind—pressure and priority.

Pressure on today's families is relentless. Sandwich-generation parents are caught between children's needs and the moral responsibility of caring for their parents. Moms and dads are programmed to meet career demands, child care, PTA meetings, social commitments and other events—driven by the need to broaden their children's horizons. Meanwhile, concern mounts over children's repeated exposure to immoral TV and questionable hero worship. Added to this are day-to-day financial pressures.

Life's priorities have had a significant impact on family relationships. On one hand, many parents have little reservation investing in cars or trips, but object to tuition hikes or school levies. Parents moving up the career ladder often ignore children who prefer time with mom and dad to material gifts. Subject to the demands of a "calendar god" which schedules time away from children, parents often awake too late to find that their kids have traded youth for eyeshadow and condoms.

Pressures and priorities are major reasons why families break up. As a result of the increasing number of broken homes, society has broadened its definition of family. However, teaching traditional family values to children is important regardless of a family's makeup.

If traditional refers to a home with a father, stay-at-home mother, and two kids, then indeed you aren't eligible. But, the term traditional reaches beyond demographics. Traditional implies a conservative childraising philosophy. A traditional parent provides favorable childhood memories. "Dates" with a parent, report card reviews, volunteerism, sacrifice, discipline, unscheduled weekend getaways, and family prayer represent typical traditional childhood gifts.

Why the hullabaloo? Contrary to what most parents believe, intellectuals, politicians, and media personalities suggest that raising children is too important to leave solely to parents. By blurring family definitions and family values, these individuals hope to have a say in how your children should be raised.

Family and future are interchangeable. The question is: Will family be in the future?

Danika

---

5 February

Dear Vasya:

Let's set the record straight. There are thousands of single parents who are raising happy, responsible children. Conversely, there are thousands of children from two-parent homes who qualify as dysfunctional. Ignore terms like traditional. The label is faded and worn only in the minds of Ozzie and Harriet groupies.

Further, the National Commission on Children asked parents to rate the condition of families and parenting in America. Respondents replied that it's harder to be a parent today than it used to be (88%) and that parents today are often uncertain about what the right thing to do is in raising their children (86%). And finally, parents don't spend enough time with their kids (81%).

The Commission, led by thirty-four distinguished Americans, including John D. Rockefeller, Dr. Barry Brazelton, and the then governor, Bill Clinton, published their report in June 1991. One of their most critical revelations was "regardless of family structure, or income, the traditional (that word again) routines of family life are increasingly being challenged by the demands of work, children's extracurricular activities, and the lure of interests and opportunities outside the home."

You can't go it alone. That's why support systems exist to help parents raise children. Companies with parental leave, schools with latchkey programs, television sit-coms featuring single parenthood situations, court rulings favoring creative family alternatives, and governmental entitlement programs are all there to assist you.

Experts recognize your family is part of the human family. If they can help empower your children, all families and the institutions that serve them will benefit.

You know what family is and why it's important. More important, you now understand how professionals can help raise your children.

Darcee

---

8 February

Dear Darcee and Danika:

After sharing your thoughts with other parents, a lively discussion ensued. One key issue kept surfacing—family values.

Assuming we accept the suggestion that undue pressures are accountable for parental and family problems, and that some outside help is necessary, how can we be sure that our children's moral structure will remain intact?

Related to this issue is family anatomy; that is, what impact will "modern" families (i.e., unmarried parents, lesbian couples) have on children?

Please be frank.

Vasya

---

11 February

Dear Vasya:

I don't mean to be pessimistic, but I must begin this letter reminding parents that there are "no guarantees in life." Hence, you can't be sure that the values and morals you teach your children will be reinforced by others.

But, there's a bright side to this situation. Consider your time constraints. You can only do so much. You can't be expected to raise your kids every minute of every day. When they leave for school, other influences come into play. Kids on the bus, teachers, playmates, and after-school caretakers will all have an impact on your child's development.

Granted, not all encounters encourage your value system, but many will, especially from authorities.

Conversely, your child transfers your value system to other children. And knowing how parents struggle, isn't it reassuring to know that you can influence those other kids.

Author, Richard Louv raises the same issue. "To whom do children turn when their parents do not have enough time for them? To other time givers, some benign, some not so benign. To peers, to gangs, to early sex partners, to the new electronic bubble of computers and video. Or if, they're lucky, to a wider web of kin, neighbors and teachers."

Louv and other experts point out that divorce is common, as is out-of-wedlock childbirth. This situation demands society reach out and support, or where appropriate, adjust the values of our children. By the way, this service must also be available for the children of two-parent "traditional" homes.

Let me give you an example of how children can grow beyond your control. Imagine a situation where your child has a new playmate whose mother spends a great deal of time volunteering at the local soup kitchen. Though you may find this value admirable, your schedule does not permit participation. Should this mother call to invite your son or daughter to join her children in this activity, you would likely be most appreciative. Why? Because your child will learn a new value that you don't have time to teach.

Suppose this mother, who gave her time to help others, never married, or conceived her child from a sperm bank. What if she was lesbian? Do you think any of these scenarios matter to the families who are being fed?

Family values, like family anatomy, can change. And in these challenging times, change can only be positive.

Darcee

11 February

Dear Vasya:

Your colleagues hit the nail on the head. You can't trust that other authorities, parents, or institutions will honor the values and morals you have given your children.

Decisions are made every day, from Washington to Hollywood, irrespective of your family values. These decisions filter down to schools, neighborhoods, even to the privacy of your own home. Unfortunately, single parents are most vulnerable to these dictates.

Vigilance is mandatory. It is especially crucial with young children, as they have not yet learned to discern adult desires. Compounding this situation is the changing definition of family, or, as you stated, anatomy.

Bizarre things are happening as courts increasingly allow family "mutations" that diminish the institution's historical contributions. When a state Supreme Court Justice could not be influenced by "fictitious legal distinctions" like a marriage certificate or an adoption order to determine what is a family, this country is in trouble. When two gay men with no children are classified as a family, the family is in trouble. When the judicial system accepts that a group of male college student renters can be a family, we're all in trouble.

In essence, two or more individuals living under the same roof, regardless of sexual orientation, marital or child status, may well acquire the same entitlements and legal respect your family has earned. Given the current political climate this may well include prisoners, army squads, rock bands, and even pedophiles who live together. George Orwell was right when he said, "There are some ideas so preposterous that only an intellectual could believe them."

No doubt the values these nontraditional "families" dignify, clash with the vast majority of America's families.

But, let's use modern examples. Would you sleep well knowing that unmarried parents, singles who choose sperm bank alternatives, and lesbian couples had the authority to teach your children morals?

Vasya, vigilance is mandatory. Teach your children morals and they will learn to avoid the immoral. Teach your children to discern and they will learn whom to trust.

Danika

Part IV
Professors and Prophets

A child is . . . a person who is going to carry on what you have started. He is going to sit where you are sitting, and when you are gone, attend to those things which you think are important. He will assume control of your cities, states and nations. He is going to move in and take over your churches, schools, universities and corporations. All of your books are going to be judged, praised or condemned by him. The fate of humanity is in his hands.

—Abraham Lincoln

---

11 February

Dear Darcee and Danika:

I guess we are a traditional family. I am a full-time wife and mother while Hasheem works as a carpenter supporting four children ages six through fifteen.

Raising children is difficult enough without worrying which parenting expert, neighbor, teacher, or relative is giving the best advice. This situation is especially sensitive when the subject is values or discipline.

How do we choose the best moral advice needed to support our parenting style? What credentials do we look for?

Brina & Hasheem

14 February

Dear Brina and Hasheem:

Selecting expert advice is challenging. Other parents will rush to your aid with their remedies. Priests will step outside their confessional, while various "tough love" authors suggest a strict code of moral discipline regardless of skyrocketing child abuse.

Let's consider criteria which should be used to select the appropriate childrearing professional.

First, training. What are their academic credentials? Degrees in child psychology, therapy or medical sciences generally indicate an understanding of child/adolescent behavior.

Second, are they published? Do they write syndicated columns or appear as a regular guest on the talk show circuit? Are they asked to give keynote speeches at professional meetings?

Examining the lay person demands a much more careful analysis. As you pointed out in your letter, neighbors, teachers, relatives, etc., are all candidates. The key is finding individuals who are both progressive and well-read. Ideal examples include adults who are tolerant, non-judgmental, and resistant to forcing values down the throats of children. Parents who avoid physical discipline while fostering an independent spirit can only strengthen the child's drive to maturity.

As your children reach adolescence, look for advisors whose attitudes, beliefs, and opinions allow for growth in decision making. The choice is especially critical in areas of sexuality, academics, spirituality, politics, and cultural diversity.

Avoid parents whose doctrine is derived from "weekend religion." Those who use the "S" (sin) word are disruptive, even dangerous. These Bible-bearing radicals will be the first to condemn your parenting style while preaching non-judgmental morality. Parenting prophets want to control your children and the world they live in. Don't let their values override all you've worked for.

Raising children is everybody's business. That's why professionals long for the day when this country has but a single educational model, discipline code, sex education curriculum, religious philosophy, diversity doctrine, social conscience, and parental protocol.

On that day parents across this country won't have to ask, "Whom do we trust?" The answer will be evident as we finally settle on a single morality designed to protect the family.

                                                        Darcee

---

                                    14 February

Dear Brina and Hasheem:

Whom do you trust? The answer used to be easy. Policemen, teachers, tele-evangelists, doctors, even lawyers were trustworthy. How the world has changed. Some policemen are burned out, teachers are unqualified, preachers are only after the almighty dollar, and doctors and lawyers are insensitive to the human spirit.

There was a time when parents could trust any of the aforementioned professionals. Today, even institutional figureheads like a Boy Scout Leader must be watched. Why? Because your kids are not their kids. The same can be said for the friendly neighbor or loving relative. Though all these "experts" are willing to guide your parenting style, none of them will be around when their wisdom bears fruit in later years.

Watch talk show programs. Psychologist "A" says, "Never spank your kids! It's child abuse." Psychologist "B" says, "Today's parents have been too lenient with children. It's time to use the rod!"

Whom do you trust? Who knows your child better than you? Who was present when the situation called for parental involvement? Who better understands the individual temperament of your children? And who, outside your home knows what values and morals you've stressed?

Think of the times when you took your young child to the pediatrician only to be told that you were overreacting. Two days and thirty dollars later your original suspicions were confirmed.

How many parents have been told by a neurologist that their child has attention deficit disorder only to learn the problem was really a bad teacher?

In his book *Back To The Family*, Dr. Raymond Guarendi took a very different approach to parental advice. Instead of telling his readers what they should or shouldn't do, he elected to share what other parents did—parents who were judged to be outstanding role models. Examples of their advice: "Initially we read books by the experts. After our first child we junked the books and relied on our intuition and our backgrounds to raise our children." Or, more simply, "I didn't rely heavily on what the experts said. I thought some of them were full of kidney beans." And more subtly, "Mary read everything that was ever published! She drove me crazy with Dr. Spock. There was a time when I could have punched him out." As Dr. Guarendi said, "Parenthood belongs first in the hands of parents. It always will."

Whom do you trust? Trust who the prophets trusted. Only then will your children follow the values their parents gave them.

Danika

---

17 February

Dear Darcee and Danika:

You will note from the enclosed correspondence that your opinions differed. That's good. Opposing views will keep our parents on their toes.

Darcee, though there may be times when parents must seek advice from others, it is generally not preferred. Such

requests may advertise weakness, or worse yet, incompe-
tence. Still, you favored expanding parental responsibility
to include professionals whose credentials confirm
childraising expertise. We also noted your caution to avoid
"Bible-bearing radicals," clergy or otherwise. In either case,
do you really feel that outside "experts" can play a significant role supporting parents? Also, please elaborate on
your "parental protocol" comment.

Danika, assuming we accept the premise that we should
rely on intuition more than guest show celebrities, books,
videos, and the like, what steps can we take to avoid having to "pick and choose" parenting partners? What resolutions should we enact which will protect the moral investment in our children?

Brina & Hasheem

---

20 February

Dear Brina & Hasheem:

"Picking and choosing" childraising authorities, not to
mention friends and neighbors, is never easy. There was
a time when parents would simply lean over their picket
fence and converse with neighbors. Parents would stroll
down the street responding to front porch invitations to
discuss the latest parental theories.

Unfortunately, today there are few picket fence or front
porch conversations. Kids aren't playing stickball while
parents share the latest discipline strategy or homework
motivation technique. Children are now locked behind
closed doors searching for computer outlets or TV control
boxes.

Meanwhile, parents spend another evening cocooning
with only phone or electronic interruptions permitted.

With so little time to raise children, moms and dads
run the risk of future encounters with authorities.

Given these pressures, the question is not so much
how to "pick and choose" as how to escape from this

rushed world, avoiding ringing phones, beeping pagers, and a chiming doorbell. Even a family drive can be interrupted by the car phone.

What are the solutions? How do parents protect the gift of childhood? Consider the following resolutions:

FAMILY INVESTMENT: When looking at financial resources, we typically think of savings accounts and home equity. But, a family investment calls for a careful audit to ensure that dollars spent on ourselves, our home, and our children, are indeed assets—not liabilities.

Another investment is time. Any function excluding children should be carefully weighed to ensure that family time won't be diminished. For working parents this might include assessing social functions and volunteer activities which, though important, can clutter calendars and over-commit exhausted parents. Parents who are actively involved in school and community functions should consider a resolution to ensure that family time is not sacrificed for friendships.

The family investment resolution takes a position that the calendar will not rule. Parents could set strict criteria ensuring that any scheduled event pass a family review. If the activity doesn't add value to your family, then perhaps the activity should be optional. Such a resolution forces parents to ask whether they're spending too much time away from their children. If the answer is yes, then moms and dads can politely decline, or reschedule a time which is not cluttered with non-family commitments.

FAMILY VALUES: The primary purpose of this resolution is to determine what is really important to children, and to identify what your family stands for and against. For instance, you may want to talk about heroes, providing kids with definitions and characteristics. This will challenge parents to offer choices to children beyond the rock star, baseball player, and financier mystique. The same criteria used to identify a hero can be used for family values.

FAMILY DIET: This is not a diet to lose weight; rather, to reduce the weighing down of young minds by too much TV and other entertainment. The challenge is to turn the TV off for a few hours a week to avoid certain programs and movies. This resolution's payback will come when children share memories of their parents and grandparents, and the time spent together.

FAMILY ADVOCACY: Wouldn't it be nice if we could teach children to be young advocates for kids? Could we expose them to children less fortunate than they, by inviting them to work at homeless shelters? Could parents show children how to write congressmen about issues which impact other families? This resolution will help raise youngsters who appreciate what they have. And perhaps it will empower youth to stand up for causes they believe in.

FAMILY TREATY: What if you formed an alliance with parents who have values similar to your own—people you can trust? Why not provide your children with the peace of mind that, when needed, other responsible parents will lend a helping hand? Treaties with other families provide a sense of security and help lessen the "stranger-danger syndrome" in children.

FAMILY PRAYER: Remember the line: " Families who pray together, stay together."

Danika

---

20 February

Dear Brina & Hasheem:

Too many parents find it difficult trying to balance community support with trust. Can they trust the neighbor to watch their kids? Will the teacher honor their values? Will the coach understand parental reservations about "get-in-your-face" aggression?

What happened to the time when you didn't have to sift through Halloween candy before consumption? Or didn't have to run stranger-at-the-door drills? Everyone is a stranger until you (or your child) get to know them. This doesn't mean they can't be trusted. Nor does it suggest that every stranger is out to destroy your child's morals.

By avoiding strangers we have eliminated a potential resource in times of danger. Consider the following scenario: Your young daughter missed the school bus. It's late, the teachers are gone and a thunderstorm is approaching. A school board member sees your child in distress and calls your home. There's no answer. Now what? If he offers your daughter a ride home will she accept or reject his invitation? Will you scold her for missing the bus or accepting a ride from a stranger?

Repeating an earlier statement, "Raising children is everybody's business." Every parent recalls an outstanding neighbor, teacher, coach, and even a relative whose handling of children was above reproach. The only difference between these people and the thousands of others who would be willing to help is that the latter are strangers. And, because you don't know them, the tendency is to not trust them. Is that fair?

Danika's paranoia is unfounded. Many parents and kids have been helped by a neighbor, teacher, coach, parenting columnist, or child psychologist. Everyone has a responsibility to help raise children. As Roman scholar Pliny the Elder stated, "What we do to our children, they will do to society." Said another way, society is accountable for raising children. Don't let fear or lack of trust stand in the way of what's best for your child's community.

Speaking of community, I'd like to address "parental protocol." Wouldn't it be nice if parents followed a proven child-raising curriculum? Imagine having a "parental cookbook" which would allow parents to flip to a section on disciplining children. How about a self-esteem section? If parents were trained to follow an approved procedure, there would be no conflicting child-raising methodologies.

Parental protocol training could be offered to new parents and mandated by the state, ensuring that all children are raised according to one set of parenting principles.

If everyone from parents to counselors, educators to court officials, followed the same parenting protocol, there would be less child abuse.

Though this country is a ways from implementing "parenting protocols," parents must be prepared to adapt to evolutionary curriculums.

Darcee

---

22 February

Dear Mir, Montana Parent's Group:

Over the past seven weeks you have had the opportunity to submit parenting questions to our consultants, Darcee and Danika. I have reviewed their responses to your questions. Your group may want to further ponder the following issues.

ON THE FIFTIES: Was this indeed a better era for raising children? Knowing there were social problems, does this in any way negate the fact that there were far fewer youths in trouble than there are today? If the weakening of our moral fiber is not the reason for forty years of decline, then what are the reasons?

ON THE NUMBERS: How do we explain increasing media and federal agency reports on crime, prison reform, safe neighborhood programs, and addiction of youth to drugs, sex, and violence? Why, if these "facts" are so unbelievable, or, unlikely to touch our children, are more and more parents suspicious of strangers? Why do more parents attend safe-home block meetings, pull kids out of public schools, or experience heightened anxiety when their children leave the house? Why do parents enter into frequent discussions with other parents on antisocial behavior, school discipline problems, news reports of adolescent rape, murder, drugs, and abuse? If the trends are false, why all the fuss?

ON VALUES AND MORALS: If we accept that laws are derived from Judeo-Christian morals, then does it follow that morals, like laws, are not guidelines? Further, can anyone honestly argue that integrity, responsibility, compassion, self-discipline, etc., fall outside the "whose values, yours or mine" argument? Beyond love, is there any greater gift we can give our children than a moral foundation? If not, doesn't the word foundation suggest bedrock—the ability to withstand temptations?

ON TRADITION: If "traditional" is a state of mind, then why do so many parents pass customs and rituals on to their children? If change is inevitable, then why do so many adults cling to the past? Why do so-called progressives fear tradition? Why do traditionalists fear those who proclaim the need for new parenting approaches to childhood? Do we not have centuries of experience to learn from? On the other hand, didn't Jesus come to change the world, to provide a new moral code? Are traditional parents the new Pharisees?

ON TRUST: Isn't what Darcee said true—that thousands of families have been helped by parenting experts? Are we concerned that experts have their own agenda, inconsistent with the morals and values we taught our children? Is it not prudent to carefully monitor those who potentially influence children? As parents, shouldn't we be the ones who decide who can and can't be trusted?

My dearest parents, I hope these questions are helpful as you continue in search of morals.

Paul, Town Elder

Chapter Two

Rights
Responsibilities
Revolution

———— ❀ ————————————————

The defense of individual rights has reached such extremes as to make society as a whole defenseless against certain individuals. It is time in the West to uphold not so much human rights as human obligations.

—Aleksander Solzhenitsyn

Part I
The Freedom Train

Every man should be responsible to others. Nor should any be allowed to do just as he pleases, for where absolute freedom is allowed there is nothing to restrain the evil which is inherent in man.

—Aristotle

---

24 February

Dear Darcee and Danika:

These days you hear a lot about rights—children's rights, animal rights, women's rights, even prisoner's rights. With all these entitlements one can't help but wonder if responsibility is in any way attached to these demands. When we were growing up, we didn't dare demand anything.

Today's children badger parents for toys or fast food until the inevitable surrender. Adolescents pressure parents for videos without regard to ratings. Teens think they have their own Bill of Rights, including the right to think for themselves, and the right to have sex when, and with whomever, they want.

Our worry is that the tendency of parents to grant more and more freedom diminishes parental authority. How should parents balance their desire to let go with their desire to protect against freedom without responsibility?

Jan & Richard

---

27 February

Dear Jan and Richard:

It's difficult for any parent to accept their child growing up. As dependency gives way to independence, friction occurs. The key is to recognize when to let go.

Children do have rights—the right to be loved, cared for, and allowed to experience self-sufficiency. As grandparents, you watched your own children mature into responsible parents. You had to let go to achieve this. Freedoms were mandatory, especially for busy parents. As parenting time diminishes, trust must prevail. Think of the twelve-year-old who must cook and feed her younger brothers and sisters because mom is working. Consider the nine-year-old boy who has learned to drive the lawn mower because his father has little time for cutting grass. These are freedoms with responsibility.

If not for progressive parents who learned to let go, families would be in constant chaos. Many parents fail to recognize that childhood is just a life stage which will sooner or later fade into photo albums and videotapes.

In some cultures adolescent girls are betrothed while their brothers learn to run the farm and defend the family name. Children from other lands have freedoms which in this country are considered the domain of adults. Why? If kids are ready to accept accountability for their actions, why not let go? Can parents, in good faith, restrict their teenagers from experiencing love and romance when they had the same emotions at that age? Is it fair to send a boy on an errand with the car, then refuse him the car for a date? And, what's the sense of not letting your ten-year-old see an outstanding movie, because of bad language, when he hears the same words on the playground?

Janis Joplin's words ring true: "Freedom is just another word for nothing else to lose." If parents would only understand that freedom is an investment in future child-parent relationships. If that investment fails then the parent has the option to withdraw the privilege. Unfortunately, many parents live a double standard.

Adults who smoke, drink, and take drugs convey the wrong message to kids who are cautioned against such behavior. Children cannot force a parent to give up these freedoms, yet parents threaten to crucify their kids if similar behaviors are observed. Is this fair?

Better to have children who are street smart, than street victims. Only then will you be able to measure responsibility.

Darcee

---

27 February

Dear Jan and Richard:

Remember Pinocchio? He was the young boy who was lured away from the security and happiness of his home by a clever adult. This barker of freedoms offered total pleasure, free from restraint and repressive authorities. Pinocchio found out, as have hundreds of other children, that there is a stiff price for freedom without responsibility.

Remember the Prodigal Son? He exchanged his father's love for a life of pleasure, only to end up wallowing among pigs. His own brother demanded to know why such a

freedom-seeking, irresponsible brother should be allowed
to return home.

You mentioned children's rights. What about parent's
rights? Is it wrong to put limits on children whose imma-
turity can lead to trouble? Is it unfair to limit freedom of
choice when that decision is contrary to public good, family value systems, or detrimental to a child's spiritual
growth? What good parent would exchange children's
rights for parental prerogative when those rights might
endanger the child?

Let's set the record straight. The only children's rights
parents must honor are to love and protect the child. If
that means disciplining a child for his or her good—so be
it. If that means saying, NO—so be it. If that means not
following the crowd, bending to peer pressure, being la-
beled old-fashioned, living with an unhappy child—so be
it. Better to be a responsible parent than to raise an irresponsible, immoral child.

Now to your key question. How should parents balance childhood freedoms with responsibility? First, all kids
are different. Some children physically mature quicker
than others, but lag behind in emotional development.
Certain adolescents can handle the parental sex education
talk while others are better off waiting a year or two. And,
some teens can tell the difference between love and sex,
whereas too many of their peers are in love with their
hormones.

Second, childhood freedoms must be secondary to
what's good for the child, consistent with a family's values
and morals. This is not a question of child maturity. It's a
question of adult accountability. Parents are God's baby-
sitters, and as such they are accountable for their performance as guardians and nurturers.

Parents who blend common sense with love and righteousness will have a much easier time surviving the journey from childhood to adulthood. Parents who fail to in-
corporate these "letting go" requirements (common sense,

love and righteousness) will most assuredly encounter turbulence. The parents of Nazi Germany's youth indoctrination programs paid a very high price for succumbing to their children's desires. Not only did many sons and daughters turn against their parents, but some of these kids lost their lives defending an evil opposed to Judeo/Christian morality.

To love our children is to respect their right to be loved. To love our children is to teach them responsibility. Parents must never confuse the two.

Danika

---

2 March

Dear Darcee and Danika:

Darcee, you appeared to advocate childhood freedoms as a mandatory parental rule. Danika, your position was much more cautious, even admonishing parents who risk letting go too early.

Regardless of your positions, we invite both of you to review *The Troubled Journey, A Profile of American Youth*. In this document you will discover that forty-seven thousand students in grades six through twelve listed a series of personal deficits including being left home alone too much, watching too much TV, attending drinking parties, feeling too much stress, and physical or sexual abuse. These are the kids talking.

Though the frequency of these deficits varied from a low of 10 percent (sexual abuse) to a high of 58 percent (alone at home), we can't help but think that freedom without responsibility is the cause. Also note the twenty at-risk indicators, again raising the "freedom-without-responsibility" issue.

Please comment accordingly.

Jan and Richard

5 March

Dear Jan and Richard:

When adolescents and teens freely admit that they
have too much time alone or drinking parties are commonplace, parents must listen. When more than one in
five children report being stressed, parents must listen.
When 27 percent of the combined student population
reports at least one incident of physical or sexual abuse,
we must all listen.

As I read through the report, I couldn't help but notice that only six in ten students felt they received some
sort of parental discipline while only 26 percent felt their
parents were involved in their schooling. If there is no
discipline at home and no parental school involvement,
then freedom without responsibility will fester.

Consider the father who allows his teenage son or
daughter to drink socially at home. Isn't it reasonable to
predict that many teens will abuse the privilege when parents are absent? As young people have greater opportunity to be home alone, the temptation to drink, smoke, or
become sexually active will increase.

Those who scream for children's rights rarely accept
the consequences of those rights. If parents abandon parental responsibilities, they cannot reasonably expect to
raise responsible children.

Sadly, some "experts" believe that today's troubled
youth should have the right to break away from parental
shackles. According to these experts, adolescent rebellion
is most often triggered by unloving, uncaring parents.
Education professor John Holt and other intellectuals
believe children should have the right to choose their
guardians. With this freedom, Holt also recommends a
guaranteed income for every man, woman, and child.
Furthermore, he believes every child should decide whether
he or she should attend school. Nuts! This irrational thinking is the revolutionary embryo which, if left unchecked,
will spawn the destruction of the American family.

Imagine the twelve-year-old boy who suddenly announces that he's had a change of heart. Not only will he quit school, initiate sexual relations, and move out of the house, but he's decided to abandon all values his parents taught him; all this in the name of freedom; all according to the Children's Bill of Rights.

Author William Donohue illustrates such madness. "No corporal punishment is allowed anywhere in Sweden, and this has come to mean that a child can sue his parents if he is either spanked or 'humiliated.'" Donohue goes on to say, "Every child has a legal voice in family decision making, and is entitled to be heard and not overruled in divorce proceedings." Donohue concludes, "Sweden is a society where it is illegal for a father to slap his daughter, but not to have intercourse with her." Whose rights are sacred?

One final point. Do not be misled by those who argue that children who abuse freedoms are rare and insignificant. If one child in 100 is left to seek his or her own pleasures, others will be infected. Remember the proverb: "No snowflake in an avalanche ever feels responsible."

Don't bury your children in an avalanche of freedoms.

Danika

---

5 March

Dear Jan and Richard:

Thank you for sending me *The Troubled Journey: A Profile of American Youth*. I found many of the statistics both interesting and disturbing. Assuming the findings are anywhere near accurate, the reader can only conclude that children's rights emanate from parental responsibility. Less than half of the forty-seven thousand students felt they had received some degree of parental communication. If mothers and fathers are too busy to take the time to talk with their kids, then other substitutes must fill the void. These typically include neighbors, peers, teachers, and other authorities. Again, I stress, this is not alarming. Kids need the freedom to bond with adults and peers who can fill their emotional needs.

I also noted that only 45 percent of students reported having a positive self-esteem. Clearly, these kids need to network beyond the home environment if they ever hope to strengthen their own self-image.

An example of networking can be found among young women who have just given birth. It isn't long before they have a strong desire to return to work to continue their careers. In fact, many experts warn women to avoid the "bonding trap" between mother and baby. On one hand, friends and relatives may suggest that a mother's place is in the home, often resulting in loss of income and advancement opportunities. On the other hand, workmates might encourage a new mother to avoid the emotional anguish of leaving her baby. But, the benefits of returning to work outweigh the drawbacks, as child care options, progressive employers, and support groups help mothers learn to balance the demands of workplace and motherhood.

Though some students from the study were heading for trouble, many more were leading commendable lives or experiencing normal adolescent folly. How many adults told their parents everything they did as kids? How many drank, smoked, skipped school, never used seatbelts, got into fights, saw a skin flick, or lost their virginity in the back seat of a car? These activities represent rites of passage from adolescence through the teenage years. What's changed is that today's successful parents realize that independence is far more important than obedience; self-expression more crucial than self-discipline.

There is a saying, "If parents haven't learned something from experience, they can always learn it from their children." Kids mirror our parental performance. If trouble blooms, parents must ask themselves: Have we failed to trust our children? Have we invaded their privacy? Have we demanded loyalty while failing to earn their respect? Have we disciplined them at the expense of self-esteem?

Have we failed to let go, choosing instead to ignore their rights and the cultivation of their freedoms?

If parents are God's baby-sitters, then children belong to God—not parents. And, like our first parents, Adam and Eve, children must have the freedom to choose.

Darcee

Part II
Cornucopia Kids

Material abundance without character is the surest way to destruction.

—Thomas Jefferson

---

5 March

Dear Darcee and Danika:

We are concerned about the effect of materialism on children. Everywhere we turn someone is promoting something to kids. Celebrities endorse everything from shoes to Disneyworld. Cartoon sponsors peddle junk food. Hollywood promotes the latest action hero, and adolescents and teens are bombarded with an array of fashion products designed to stimulate hormones.

If this isn't enough, media personalities impose their values on youth, often destroying what parents worked hard to instill.

What steps should we take to protect children from those who would sell their souls to entice our kids?

John and Ronica

---

8 March

Dear John and Ronica:

I don't envy parents who have to scrutinize every ad, commercial, or product display. It's tough enough raising kids without baby-sitting an entire industry.

But, with so many candy bars, fashions, cosmetics, movies, toys, video games, sporting goods, recordings, computer software, athletic shoes, cereals, colas, hamburgers, toothpaste brands . . . . well, you get the picture. Parents cannot monitor every purchasing decision made by their kids. Fortunately, there are safeguards like the Consumer Product Safety Commission, the Children's Television Act and parental warning labels. In addition, friends, neighbors, and teachers can help safeguard children. Even your child's peers can have a positive impact when they steer them away from inappropriate products or services.

Parents can put their minds at ease if they learn to accept the following truths.

1. The vast majority of items marketed to kids will have little or no effect on the values you have given your children. If anything, parental values should act as the shock absorber during the child's journey to adulthood.

2. Market demand will determine which "kid concepts" survive. Questionable fashion, lyrics, or movie content will fade as children become adolescents and adolescents become teens.

3. Sophisticated kids make sophisticated buyers. As a child matures, he or she will offset fads and peer pressure with a more conservative purchasing behavior. Pet rocks have long been buried.

4. Government authorities will never permit inappropriate products or services on the market because of pressure from family watchdog groups. Furthermore, companies appeal to children whose emotional or physical development is compatible with their business. Failure to do so would be financial suicide.

5. When Coke squares off against Pepsi, McDonald's against Burger King or Reebok against L.A. Gear, only reputable spokespersons are used. That's why entertainment and sports stars are recruited.

6. Advertising is nothing more than education. With this knowledge children will learn how to discern the true value being offered.

7. Trusting children to do the right thing is essential in building a positive relationship between parents and kids. Parents must guide but never demand. Children whose parents guide rather than demand are more likely to become responsible adults.

8. Materialism is self-policing. If kids don't have money, they can't buy.

9. There will be times when parents should set aside their fears about raising a materialistic child, because most peer groups will have similar tastes. Forcing your child to dress differently or succumb to your musical preferences will only hurt his self-esteem.

10. There is hardly a better way to respect children's rights than to give them the freedom to learn from their own purchasing behavior. Remember Joplin's words, "Freedom is just another word for nothing else to lose."

The issue is not how to protect children from evil marketers, but how to cope with thirty-second sound bites, impersonal displays, untouchable images, cryptic lyrics or a cluttered mailbox.

Remember, materialism is nothing more than a product of technology designed for a higher standard of living. And, if we really want a better world for our kids, then freedom from overprotective parents is our only choice.

Darcee

---

8 March

Dear John and Ronica:

Protecting children appears to be the number one parental priority. It used to be education, teaching values, or ensuring good health. Times have changed. The battle facing parents can overwhelm even the most devoted mothers and fathers.

How can parents fight drugs, violence, and valueless education, yet protect their kids from seven billion dollars of corporate advertising? This investment in youth continues to escalate as younger and younger children gain purchasing power. Designer fashions, non-nutritious foods, $200 "pumps" for the $300 basketball camp are examples of the kinds of pressures parents face.

The Madison Avenue classification for kids with cash is: SKIPPIES (school kids with income and purchasing power). Experts realize that children exert tremendous pressure on parents to buy.

It's not just a matter of marketing products to youth. It's also a question of stealing their childhood. Do ten year olds need lipstick or eye shadow? Should Jordache jeans be the catalyst for young girls to go on diets? Should banks court kids with credit card offers?

Be careful of the freedoms you offer your children. The price for buying their approval could be costly. Don't rush high heels, nylons, or designer clothes. Don't ignore music lyrics or motion picture ratings. Recognize that those cute action figures at your child's favorite fast food restaurant are often violent superheroes. Accompany your kids to the library, checking out what they check out. As for adolescents, point out that the BMW kids on "90210" are beyond the reach (thank God!) of 99 percent of the population.

Don't allow your children to be swayed by advertising jingles or slogans. "Have it your way," "Be all that you can be," "You can be anything you want," "You deserve a break today," "Who says you can't have it all." These are potentially dangerous messages. The overriding theme is narcissism—the love of self. This is not self-esteem. It's self-indulgence.

Discernment is the key to protecting children from "pleasure island." Teach them how to differentiate right from wrong—real from unreal. Youth who learn to apply their parents' values will likely engage in proper behavior. Children who are taught moderation will avoid overindulgence. And, young adults who learn to stand strong in their beliefs (as learned from their parents) will not fall victim to peer pressure.

As children, you must teach them. As adolescents, you must guide them. As teens, you must pray for them.

Danika

---

11 March

Dear Danika and Darcee:

Some of us see avoiding materialism as an insurmountable task in a world where bumper stickers proclaim, "He who dies with the most toys wins." Other parents have renewed their commitment to avoid spoiling children.

Darcee, your final comment suggests that only liberal parents want a better world for kids. Surely, protective parents may qualify for that same wish. Doesn't unlimited freedom, or freedom at too young an age, set the stage for parental heartbreak?

Danika, it seems to us that Darcee's comment on "trust" may well contradict your "protective" position. Sooner or later kids will make choices about how they dress, what they listen to, what movies they see, etc. How do we balance our right to parent our children with their right to grow up?

Please critique each other's commentary.

John and Ronica

---

14 March

Dear John and Ronica:

When I caution against overprotective parents, I am drawing a parallel to mothers and fathers who trust no one—not friends, neighbors, teachers, or relatives. Some are so extreme that they refuse to own a television or allow their kids to date. Fear is their first weapon, punishment their second.

To be liberated does not suggest that children should be allowed to buy anything that pleases them. Remember my statement, "Parental values should act as the shock absorber during the child's journey to adulthood." If parents point their kids in the right direction, there will be little to worry about.

It's like teaching a child to swim. No loving parent would push their kid off the dock and yell, "Go ahead, you're free to swim." The parent would first teach the child how to swim. Once that's accomplished, the child should be allowed to experience his new-found freedom. This is letting go.

Most parents are born with a protective spirit. The key is to know when to release that energy. This leads to your question about freedom leading to parental heartbreak.

How many times have we heard about children whose overprotective parents caused them to run away, led to adolescent pregnancy, manifest multi-color hair, a pierced nose ring, or bizarre tattoo? Don't you think these kids' parents have broken hearts?

Given the opportunity to do over, most parents of rebellious youth would choose another battle. If they could turn the clock back they would gladly spoil their children. This is not "buying their approval."

Interestingly, Danika admonishes parents who fail to teach children how to discern what the kids should, and should not, invest in. If experience is the best teacher, how can one profit from mistakes if not allowed to fail?

As Madonna says, "We live in a material world." There is no getting around it. Kids are going to be exposed to thousands of commercials. They are going to experience peer pressure, eventually leading to a crisis with mom and dad. They are going to buy the wrong product, get taken in a "deal," succumb to fads, and grow up faster than parents wish. It has always been so.

Why fight it? There will be many more things to worry about than violent Power Rangers or sexy Barbie dolls.

Just a generation ago the thought of leaving children home alone was unthinkable. Today, kids as young as ten are cooking dinner, cleaning house, and watching siblings. This freedom allows mom to have a career, thereby fulfilling her promise to provide the children with a higher standard of living.

There are many parents in the world who pray they might be in a position to spoil their children. And freedom is just another way to achieve this goal.

Darcee

---

14 March

Dear John and Ronica:

Trust must be earned. Look carefully at Darcee's position. "Parents must guide but never demand," she states. Yet, how can parents teach responsibility without teaching consequences for irresponsibility? If parents are only guides responsible for pointing children in a particular direction, then who will be accountable for actions taken by kids who choose the wayward path?

If parents sacrifice the right to overrule their children's actions for fear of being overprotective, then society might as well abandon all codes of conduct.

The right to parent our children must never take a backseat to youth's impatience to grow up. Only mom and dad can decide when their child is ready for certain freedoms.

Balancing parental control with a child's developing independence depends on the parents' expectations for that child. If he or she has demonstrated responsibility, including the ability to handle peer pressure, more freedom is in order. Remember Jesus' parable about the master who gave three servants a limited amount of talents to invest in his absence. Two servants invested wisely, while the third proved incapable of handling the task. The inept servant was punished, while the other two were given greater accountability. Mold your children first. Worry about their rights later. Your children will thank you.

Allow me to comment on Darcee's so-called "truths." First, children of all ages are impressionable. Peer pressure and constant anti-family messages will (if not checked) eventually influence kids. Second, inappropriate products, services, or themes may not brainwash all kids, but those who are susceptible will have an impact on other children. Third, the pet rock may be dead, but the Grateful Dead and similar groups are not. Fourth, if you trust the government and profit-motivated companies to do what's right, you run the risk of washing childhood down a moral sink. Fifth, how many entertainment or sports personalities would you trust to teach values to your child? Sixth, the primary goal of advertising is to influence behavior—not to educate. Seventh, children must earn your trust. Eighth, materialism is self-indulgence—not self-policing. And finally, freedom is just another word for everything to lose.

Danika

Part III
"Gonna Do It Anyway"

Everything is sliding downhill. Captains of industry cheat on government contracts, bankers knowingly violate security laws, politicians accept contributions that are just short of bribes. In the midst of moral collapse our society responds literally and metaphorically by passing out condoms.

—James J. Kilpatrick

14 March

Dear Darcee and Danika:

I'm one of several single parents who will soon be raising teenagers. One of our greatest worries is the increasingly common sexual promiscuity among today's youth. Just the other day one of our parents intercepted a letter from a fourteen-year-old girl which made us all blush. Here are some excerpts:

"I lust after your thick muscular body. I'd love to run my fingers through your soft curly brown hair and take long meaningful lust gazes into your brownish-green eyes.

Kissing your soft, luscious, sexy lips is my first goal and after that I'd like to seduce you till you drop!"

If I ever wrote a letter like that and my mother got hold of it, I wouldn't be around to write this letter.

What's happening? Are hormones different? Are parents different? How do we protect our kids' virginity—or is it our place to do so?

Vasya

---

17 March

Dear Vasya:

No, hormones aren't different. As for parents, well that's another story. Many parents are so caught up in the pressures of work and raising children, there's little time to monitor the sexual behavior of their kids. Some parents have surrendered common sense to the sexual appetites of youth.

A recent talk show featured parents who allowed their teenagers to have sex in their home. The parents' rationale was that kids are going to do it anyway, so let's be sure they are taking precautions in the safety of their own environment. This philosophy gives new meaning to the term "sleepover."

Vasya, as a single parent you probably won't be surprised to know that some adults justify their liberal attitude because they have little time to watch their kids. Another reason frequently used is that single parents have overnight dates, so criticizing their teenager for extra-marital sex is hypocritical.

This logic is supported by television's "everybody does it" mentality. Music lyrics rap "let's do it," and Nike chants "just do it." It isn't long before friends enter the fray with, "we just did it and it's great!"

Regrettably, the entertainment industry and peer groups are not the only spheres of influence. More and more schools are passing out condoms to "protect" kids. Respected magazines print articles proclaiming, "You're

mom was wrong. Sex is the most important thing in life!"
And, experts like Dr. Ruth are delighted when teen callers
confirm condom usage during intercourse. The good doctor is quick to counsel, "there are no limits" to sexual
gratification.

Everywhere kids turn, sex is thrown at them. Waking
up to rock lyrics is followed by health classes focusing on
reproduction. When kids return home, TV's soap stars are
hopping in and out of bed. Springer, Jones, Donahue,
and Geraldo, among others, feature transsexuals, nym-
phomaniacs, and mothers who allow their daughters to
have sex at home. The evening news recites one sexual
pathology after another. Following are "Current Affair"
programs which report the latest celebrity sexual harassment case. Finally, the prime-time movie coaches the
adolescent who earlier was titillated by the thirty-second
promo promising seduction, violence, and plenty of skin.

These impressions are absorbed by adolescents at a
time when hormones are boiling. The days have long since
passed when a sneak preview of dad's Playboy or the catalog underwear section satisfied the sexual curiosity of youth.
All kids have to do is go to a movie, turn on the TV, or
buy comic books targeted at mature readers.

Author William Donohue says it best. "Raging hormones is surely an expression of the 80's, but it no more
accurately describes a phenomenon of youth today than in
the past; hormones raged with just as much intensity among
young people in the fifties, the difference being, however,
that social pressure kept them from being recklessly ven-
tilated."

"They're going to do it anyway." Is that true? Are kids
absolutely, positively going to have sex in their adolescent
or teen years? If so, why are so many young people virgins? Why are abstinence programs springing up everywhere?

It is not only your place, but your obligation to protect
your children. Failure to accept this responsibility will only
result in greater numbers of kids contracting sexually transmitted diseases, now at three million.

Parents must be aggressive in their fight to raise morally conscious children. They must establish values protecting the integrity of adolescent and teen sexuality. They must be vigilant in guarding childhood, refusing to accept immoral television, movies, music, and other mediums which can seduce kids. And, they must get actively involved with positive programs which promote abstinence, virtue, and respect.

In the coming years your children will naturally challenge your resolve to continue their moral training. Be firm. Be consistent. Be loving.

Danika

---

17 March

Dear Vasya:

It is not the place of parents to protect the virginity of their kids anymore than it is their place to tell kids what religion they should adopt. But, it is a parent's place to reach out to youth who want to learn about and experience their human sexuality.

To give you an idea how desperate kids are, consider that in a medium size Midwestern town, more than 15,600 calls were made to a teen tape program in a single year. Many requested tapes had something to do with sex, love, or body changes.

"Myths About Sex," "How Can Pregnancy Be Prevented," "Rape: What Should I Know," and "How Do I Know If I Am In Love" were the most popular tapes. "My Body Changes: His/Hers," something you would think parents would discuss with their kids, was the eighth most popular tape. Sadly, more than four hundred kids requested the tape "My Parents Don't Understand Me."

Consequences of parental failure often cause adolescents to enter into a relationship unprepared to handle sexual activity. In a national survey of seventh to ninth graders, 65 percent of boys and 46 percent of girls under the age of fifteen felt that it was okay to be raped or to rape your date after six months of steady dating.

Where are these kids' parents? If young people are going to engage in sexual experimentation, (and most will) parents must play a role. If kids are going to risk disease and possible death, parents must try to actively protect them from themselves. Youth fear nothing. Parents must fear for them.

Abstinence, condoms, and related discussions must begin in the home. Other qualified authorities will also help through school mandated sex education curricula and network specials promoting a safe-sex message. Some misinformed groups will try to convince parents that their only responsibility is to steer kids away from any message other than total abstinence. That would be like telling your son or daughter never to drive a car because of the high risk among teen drivers. You know teens are going to drive just as you know they're going to have sex. You also know that if your teenager refuses to wear a seatbelt, there is a significantly higher chance of serious injury. The same is true of condoms. In both cases death may be the outcome.

For these reasons, it is your place to get involved—not as a virginity gatekeeper, but as counselor to your children. This call to duty is not due to some super strain of hormones. Your children's hormones are no different today than yours, mine, your parents, or grandparents were yesterday. The only difference is today's environment.

In your generation teens were intimidated by "fire and hell" sermons, educational systems which banished the girl who made a mistake and other "town without pity" chastisements. Fortunately, these old-fashioned attitudes are slowly but surely disappearing. Kids don't need lectures. They need understanding. And they don't need a "birds and bees" speech. They need sex education.

Darcee

20 March

Dear Darcee and Danika:

Both of you have succeeded in convincing us that hormones are hormones, regardless of generations. You also helped us realize that we must get involved.

What's not clear is whether we "draw a line in the sand" or merely counsel the kids on changing bodies, teenage love, and sexual activity.

On one hand, parents want to be strict about dating, on the other hand they don't want to drive their kids away. Some parents wish to be open, answering any questions their son or daughter may ask about sex and its taboos. Other moms and dads prefer to control what the kids know and when they should know it.

Please help us find common ground.

Vasya

---

23 March

Dear Vasya:

Common ground by its mere definition suggests compromise. As a youngster approaches adolescence, more "give and take" will be necessary if harmony between parent(s) and child is to occur. As an adolescent becomes a full-blooded teenager, negotiation skills for both parties will be essential.

Compromise usually results when both parties are satisfied with the deal. This generally means parents allow their son or daughter an extended privilege because that child has earned the trust. It does not require parents to submit to pressure or emotional outbursts. Further, because you are the parent, democracy is at your discretion, not the child's. You have the final say; should you choose to say "no" then so be it. Better to have an angry son or daughter than a child in serious trouble.

When they sense they're not going to get their way, children (especially teenagers) will try to get you to compromise. They are not alone. The media will compromise by selling kids safe sex through the use of condoms. Ad campaigns trumpet safe sex slogans, berating parents who continue to cling to the abstinence albatross. Hollywood and network executives justify their compromise through "prime time" hours or movie ratings. ACLU officials offer a First Amendment compromise, publicly condemning production of child pornography, while defending the pedophile's rights to purchase such materials. School officials who forbid posting the Ten Commandments legitimize their compromise before the School Board by also rejecting satanic student clubs.

Compromise is often the bridge to a permissive society. It's a way of giving in or backing off to avoid confrontation. Unfortunately, every time we take a step backwards, more and more liberties leap forward.

Why are children as young as ten discussing oral sex? Why are gang members recruited at eight years of age? Why are first-graders being taught about alternative lifestyles? Why is degrading art funded by taxpayers? Why can radio disc jockeys spew anything from their mouths while the music they play promotes cop killing, rape, and lying to parents?

Someone has compromised. Someone has failed to draw a line in the moral sand.

This lack of courage can, in a very short time, have devastating effects on our society. Authors, Dr. James Dobson and Gary Bauer state, "Pornography has now become sexually explicit. Perversions are now defined as a preference or orientation." "Pedophilia is now considered an orientation rather than a sexual deviation."

Reaching common ground does not mean parents must give ground. Parents are not counselors. They are parents. Their job is to set limits, provide a moral foundation, and, when appropriate, initiate consequences. Parents who compromise may not only lose ground, but may well lose control of their kids.

Danika

---

23 March

Dear Vasya:

I applaud you and those parents who seek common ground with their kids. It's refreshing to see parents recognize the importance of parental democracy.

Let's begin with erasing the "line in the sand" mentality. Parents who prepare for battle may lose more than a war, they may lose their kids.

How many times have you heard or read stories about runaways whose parents never listened? Those mothers and fathers chose to fight rather than negotiate. They chose to condemn rather than understand. And oftentimes they chose to punish, frequently physically, rather than forgive. The result—a broken family.

In one example, a mother and father, disgusted with their cluttered fifteen-year-old daughter's room, gave this ultimatum. "Clean your room or leave!" The daughter cleaned her room and left! Six months later the daughter returned home. The mother pointed out that if you are going to give ultimatums you'd better be prepared for the consequences.

Consider heavier issues—teen love and sexuality. How many times have you heard the story about the girl who was forbidden to date the boy she eventually married? Or how about the couple whose rebellion led to pregnancy? Worse yet, experts will tell you that many teen suicides are directly related to a lover's breakup. Sadly, such actions are often the result of confrontational parents who failed to predict the consequences of uncompromising behavior.

To avoid driving the kids away, parents should proceed with caution in discussions challenging youthful independence. Using caution does not mean parental au-

thority has no place. But, it does suggest that parental
bullying is out of place.

Vasya, you mentioned that "some parents wish to be
open, answering any questions their son or daughter may
ask about sex and its taboos." Doesn't this statement suggest that members of your own parenting group have found
an effective way to trust their children?

Consider the number of kids who are introduced to
sex by children their own age or younger. This discovery
is generally followed by embarrassing questions which
parents are uncomfortable answering.

Why go through this? Why not be up front and educate your children before some street urchin does? Knowledge should not end with the "basics," as natural curiosity
will leapfrog over "baby-making" to "pleasure seeking."

Carrying this argument further, the time will rapidly
approach when parents must graduate from "how to have
sex" to "how to protect yourself when having sex." If dad
only talks to his son about self-control without mentioning
pregnancy and disease protection, that father is irresponsible. If mother talks to her daughter about the "joys of
sex" and then tries to push abstinence, the contradiction
will blow up in her face.

If kids trust parents to answer their questions honestly, then parents must trust kids to act responsibly. Be
there for them. Answer their questions, regardless of content. And when they're ready, offer advice on how to protect themselves from disease, pregnancy, and AIDS. Not
only will you demonstrate how much you trust them, but
how much you love them.

                                                    Darcee

Part IV
Victimology and Other Entitlements

The nuns at my school made me pray when I didn't want to and I didn't know why I should; made me work when I saw no reason to; made me believe in equality of races when our country paid lip service to equality and our church tolerated inequality; and they made me accept responsibility for my own life when I looked for excuses.

—Judge Clarence Thomas
Supreme Court Justice

---

23 March

Dear Darcee and Danika:

I've got a couple of young kids who insist they have too many chores to do. "How come our friends' parents don't make them do chores?" they ask. Jokingly, I tell them that they are victims of their dad's desire to make them earn their keep. They don't understand.

It seems too many kids perceive themselves as victims. They cheat on tests, get caught, but it's not their fault. They drop out of school, but it's not their fault. They take drugs, get pregnant, marry the wrong person, but it's not their fault.

If it's not their fault, then whose fault is it? If my oldest son doesn't clean his room and I punish him by forcing him to do extra chores at the expense of playing baseball, whose fault is it if he doesn't make the team?

If I fail to do my job the way my boss expects, I'm not going to avoid the consequences because of my "victimology defense." Why should kids expect different treatment?

Gillie

25 March

Dear Gillie:

Years ago there was a concept floating around that children should be held accountable by age seven. The Catholic Church timed the Sacrament of Confession and acknowledgment of sin to this magical age.

Fortunately, mature adults recognize this "mea culpa" attitude as a direct attack on a child's self-esteem. Rational parents understand that many children are victims in this fast-paced society. Kids' pressures include drugs, teen pregnancy, getting bad grades, joining gangs, watching too much TV, seeing R-rated movies, drinking, smoking, vandalism, fighting, and missing religious services. With so many warnings, is it any wonder that youth in record numbers experience stress.

At the same time these threats hang over their heads, kids are exposed to parents, guardians, teachers, and other adults who violate the very rules children are expected to follow. Many of these same adults are bad parents who physically and emotionally abuse their children. Take for example the recent Florida case of an eleven-year-old boy who sued for his constitutional right to terminate the parent-child relationship. He said his mother was incompetent. He wants good parents and in fact has found them.

In another case, a childless couple desperately wanted to adopt a child whose teenage mother walked out of the hospital after delivery. Instead, the judge returned the child to the biological mother one month before adoption was complete. This child is a victim.

Kids who do poorly in school because of too much television are also victims, because their parents haven't stressed the importance of good grades.

When parents refuse to counsel their sexually active teenagers on condom usage and a pregnancy occurs, the victims are the kids.

Kids driven to drink, smoke, or take drugs are victimized by unloving parents. And, kids driven into poverty by economic injustice, who steal, rob, and even kill for their survival, are victims.

From *Childhood's Future*, comes this telling testimonial from a teacher. "Suicide is just aggression turned inward. These highly intelligent kids are cutting themselves with razor blades to ease the aggression they feel." The teacher further stated, "I've had kindergartners run out in traffic and try to kill themselves. Very few of the kids are actually mentally ill. Suicide isn't built into them. They're reacting to something in their family."

These kids are victims. Kids who fail are victims. Kids who commit crimes against society are victims. And kids who strike back at unfair parental discipline are victims.

In every case, we must be both tolerant and compassionate. For undoubtedly, children mirror the values adults give them. Spank a kid and he will physically punish another. Teach tolerance and the child will learn to accept others.

Gillie, you asked whose fault it is when a child fails. Only parents are accountable when youth stray. And that's why society must get involved to salvage those kids who can be saved.

Darcee

---

25 March

Dear Gillie:

Victimology is the newest parasite feeding off parents who are led to believe that troubled kids are not accountable for their actions. Victimologists will tell society that people with AIDS are victims because the government refuses to spend enough money to find a cure. They will rush to the defense of Ted Bundy types because society didn't recognize an addiction to pornography. Minorities with violent behavior are excused because they were oppressed. Dysfunctional families are victimized by functional families. And don't forget, smokers killed by cancer are victims of the tobacco industry.

The list is endless. Yet, what people forget is that many of these so-called victims, children included, were wrong. They broke the law. They lied. They stole. They sinned!

But, these "victims" feel they're above the law. They shouldn't be held accountable. It's not their fault. They're misunderstood.

Let's play out this logic. Take a ten-year-old boy who gets caught stealing a cassette. Most parents will march the little boy back to the store to meet the manager and face the music. The boy's mother and father don't see him as a victim. But, they do recognize that if they don't deal with this problem now, a judge will later.

Some "experts" will claim that the boy's self-esteem has been damaged by the humiliation suffered at the hands of parents. His folks didn't understand this consequence and now they're accountable for future misbehavior. Nonsense.

What if the kid lives in the ghetto? Does he have license to steal from other ghetto kids? If a teenage boy gets a girl pregnant, can he legitimately claim that his parents never told him about abstinence, and therefore he's not responsible? If a girl skips school and ultimately fails, is she not responsible?

The tendency to pass blame costs society dearly. A New York man who leapt in front of a subway train was awarded $650,000 because the train failed to stop before he was severely injured. In another case, a defense attorney claimed "cultural psychosis" as the reason why one inner city teenage girl killed another in a fight over a coat.

This thinking is absurd; not because youth can't be victims, but because their behavior is wrong. If teens choose to have sex and get AIDS, it is not the fault of parents who preach abstinence. If a young boy joins a gang, his parents are not accomplices.

Good parents see victimology for what it is—another alibi to avoid blame. If children are not taught to fear the consequences of their behavior, then they will not fear becoming victims of their own actions.

Danika

---

28 March

Dear Darcee and Danika:

After sharing your correspondence with our parents' group, many of them began to feel like victims. Those who saw themselves as loving parents questioned if their discipline style was, in fact, victimizing the very children they were trying to help. Most parents could, however, corroborate stories about children who are victims of broken homes. Clearly, each case must stand on its own merit.

During our discussions a related topic surfaced. The word "entitlement" has crept into our checkbooks, with citizens paying more and more taxes for government programs and mandates. Curiously, today's youth seem to feel they are entitled to a happy, healthy, wealthy lifestyle guaranteed by mom and dad.

These "birth rights" appear to reach beyond the gifts our parents gave us. Please identify entitlements parents owe their kids.

Gillie

---

31 March

Dear Gillie:

You're a single parent. After your wife passed away, you were left with the mother and father roles, responsible for raising two very young children.

You know your kids are entitled to a warm home, food on the table, a quality education, and a loving parent. You also realize that all children are entitled to receive a strong moral foundation.

That's it. Parents don't owe their kids a successful future. Dads need not promise their sons employment. Mothers do not owe their daughters one stitch of designer clothing. Teens are not entitled to a car on their sixteenth birthday, at graduation, or any other time.

In political circles, entitlement is usually a government program designed to satisfy the "rights" of citizens who are lacking access to something others have. Some children and adults are legitimately served. Unfortunately, too many recipients and their sponsors have convinced politicians that taxpayers should fund these programs. Those hired to administer the grant are grateful that so many underprivileged citizens have kept them employed. Their motto could be, "Please remain entitled so I can get paid."

Think about kids who follow a similar formula. They are pleased their parents are employed and making money, a portion of which they are entitled to. These kids believe it's their right. They learn to take, not to earn. They learn rights without responsibility. And most of all, they learn to expect their parents to provide for their needs and desires. They also expect to be bailed out when "pleasure island" leads them into trouble. After all, they're just kids who aren't responsible for their actions.

No fault. These words are not solely the property of the divorce and auto insurance industries. This philosophy has become a common defense for children who have been brought up to believe that kids are exempt from guilt. The fault lies with society, big business, government, teachers, parents, and other authorities.

Remember rebellious youth of the sixties who wouldn't trust anyone over thirty? Guess who's over thirty now? The flower children who demanded free love are now burning their bell-bottoms, crushing their granny glasses, and choking on marijuana leaves. Their kids are wild, out of control, and addicted to entitlements, rights, and freedom.

Sexual liberation has evolved to now include children as young as ten whose eight-year-old siblings are learning about masturbation, incest, and homosexuality. This new freedom is inversely related to accountability. When a teenage girl forgets her pill or a boy his condom, and pregnancy leads to abortion, liberals defend both against parental judgments by claiming they are victims of society's ills.

Birth rights go hand-in-hand with parental responsibility. Parental rights determine what entitlements children will receive—not the other way around. Remember Gillie, a warm home, food on the table, a quality education, a loving parent, and a moral foundation are all that's expected of a good parent. Anything beyond these necessities should be allocated only when children come to understand the consequences of abusing privileges.

Danika

31 March

Dear Gillie:

Entitlements result from parental failure to raise children properly. Victims of physical and emotional abuse continue the cycle with their own children, driving up the demand for social services. In addition, economic decline driven by adult greed further fuels the need for government programs.

Dysfunctional families are a growth industry. Consider the number of children who cry out for help. Kids on drugs, survivors of incest, alcoholics, bulimics, children of divorce, school dropouts, and youth with sexual and self-esteem problems all represent a growing army of victims.

These children are not to blame for their lot in life, much less their behavior. Is it not obvious that they should be entitled to the best society has to offer?

Gillie, let's look at your "birth right" objections. You stated that today's youth, "feel they are entitled to a happy,

healthy, wealthy lifestyle guaranteed by mom and dad."
What parent do you know who, given the option, wouldn't
prefer to have happy, healthy, wealthy kids? If parents
could guarantee such blessings, wouldn't they do so?

The issue bothering you seems to revolve around the
child's expectations. Let's take each component separately.

From the time children are old enough to understand
language, they are taught that loving parents want kids to
grow up happy. They learn that toys, McDonald hamburgers, movies, and Nintendo are the kinds of things that
fulfill their quest for happiness. Parents are there to satisfy their needs. Both parties understand this relationship.
As a child enters adolescence, toys and the like are replaced with more mature pleasures including PG-13 movies, stylish clothes and the latest electronic gadgetry. With
maturing teens, parents guarantee happiness through car
keys, later curfews, and parentless vacations.

When parents provide these gifts, both adult and child
are happy. Both have developed a stronger relationship
with each other.

The second entitlement is health. Again, any good
parent will give children nutritious food, encourage exercise, take them to the doctor, and bundle them up on cold
days. Children are entitled to a healthy lifestyle. This is
common sense.

Now for the third and most difficult entitlement to
grasp—wealth. We live in a materialistic society. Everywhere kids look there are reminders of the wealth this
nation has to offer. Many children grow up in homes with
three thousand plus square feet, in secluded suburbs, blocks
away from private schools. Their parents have expensive
late-model cars, go to the finest restaurants, are members
of exclusive clubs, and enjoy family getaways to exotic
resorts. These kids are given every material gift possible
and are preconditioned to receiving the best.

Parents who choose their children's lifestyles are fully
accountable for ensuring that lifestyle continues. Courts
mandate this rationale every time they award a divorcing

homemaker a significant portion of the wage-earner's salary. This ruling guarantees that the family will not suffer the loss of a certain lifestyle.

Though I've used an upscale model, the same holds true for all income levels. Kids are entitled to receive the same or greater lifestyle than that of their parents. This is what your parents wanted for you and your grandparents wanted for your parents. The cycle will continue as you demand that your children provide a better lifestyle for your grandchildren.

Hopefully, parents will realize (as the bumper sticker says) "he who dies with the most toys wins."

Darcee

---

12 April

Dear Mir, Montana Parents' Group:

This is my second letter intended to stimulate analysis of Danika and Darcee's advice.

ON FREEDOM: Is "letting go" synonymous with children's rights? Is it possible that many parents are forced to give childhood freedoms because of work and family obligations? Shouldn't responsibility be demonstrated before freedoms are granted? Can parents logically compare today's environment with other cultures or other times? If so, wouldn't tougher discipline and more stringent moral standards apply? Though Darcee makes a valid point about parents who set bad examples (i.e., viewing R-rated movies, smoking, drinking, etc.), must they relinquish adult behaviors for fear of violating equal rights for children? Are there too many childhood liberties, or is it a question of freedom?

ON PARENTAL ACCOUNTABILITY: Should parents be responsible for kids whose behavior gets them in trouble? Could it be that there are children who, like some adults, choose the wrong path? Are these kids not accountable? If parents choose to give their child independence, who's responsible for the outcome? Does it depend on the child, the situation, or the history of such actions?

ON MATERIALISM: Do kids have too much? Do they expect too much? Have they learned the value of a dollar? How about the blessings they have? Can parents realistically monitor every societal influence as they try to protect their kids from becoming materialistic. Can greed be good? Is there anything wrong with a high standard of living? Isn't that the wish of all parents? Can there be subliminal evils inherent in youth advertising or programming?

ON SEX: How is it that so many adolescents and teens have yet to trade in their virginity? Are the parents of these kids not doing their job in providing the proper sex education? Given the choice, would it not be better to have parents supply condoms rather than risk disease or death? Or, is the issue one of morals? Is sex what the kids really want or what Hollywood and the media want them to want? If kids increasingly request sex information, is this due to natural desires or societal pressures, or both? Is the "wearing a seatbelt" argument a fair comparison to the "wearing a condom" argument? Isn't there a direct correlation to fifties values and lower rates of teen pregnancy, sexually transmitted diseases; or, conversely, nineties freedoms and rampant sexuality problems?

ON COMMON GROUND: If adults are the ultimate authority in the parent/child relationship, is "common ground" a necessary directive for handling disagreements? Must parents compromise to restore order? Does "pick your own battles" suggest giving ground? Is conflict resolution a process for finding common ground, or just another way to avoid confrontation? Given the option, would parents prefer to compromise in return for family peace? Which is the greater risk—youth rebellion or youth destruction?

ON VICTIMOLOGY: Are bad kids victims? Should the school bully be understood when he taunts weaker children? If all kids are victims of their environments, why have limits, rules, consequences? Why parent? As young victims become adults, do their handicaps dissolve, or may they continue to hide behind the victimology defense? Perhaps it's only the ghetto kids who qualify for special protection. If so, then why aren't the vast majority of these children abusing the system? Could it be that their parents taught them right from wrong, with discipline the reward for those who dare to go astray? Will the teacher, truant officer, or judge absolve the child who breaks the rules? Who are the real victims of victimology?

ON ENTITLEMENTS: If entitlements are really "birth rights" then what must parents provide other than food, shelter, and love? When a youth reminds parents that he or she didn't ask to be born, does that suggest that entitlements are null and void?

My dearest parents, remember that rights without responsibilities will only result in revolution.

Paul, Town Elder

Chapter Three

Hell's Heroes

— ❁ ————————————————————————————

If we in this nation continue to sow the images of murder, violence, drug abuse, sadism, arrogance, irreverence, blasphemy, perversion, pornography, and aberration before the eyes of millions of children, year after year and day after day, we should not be surprised if the foundations of our society rot away as if from leprosy.

—Sen. Robert Byrd, Democrat
W. Virginia: Speech on Senate Floor
18 September 1991

Part I
That's Entertainment?

The winds of change blew through the dream factories of make-believe, tore at its crinoline tatters . . . the hedonists, the homosexuals, the hemophiliac bleeding hearts, the God-haters, the quick-buck artists who substituted shock for talent, all cried: "Shake em! Rattle em! God is dead. Long live pleasure! Nudity? Yea! Wife-swapping? Yea! Liberate the world from prudery. Emancipate our films from morality!" . . . There was dancing in the streets among the disciples of lewdness and violence.

—Frank Capra
Three-time Oscar Winner,
Director of *It's A Wonderful Life* 1972

12 April

Dear Darcee and Danika:

We're confused. There was a time when "entertainment" meant just that. Today, regardless of content or contribution to society, the term seems to dignify any film, song, art, program, or writing.

When we look at the messages paraded before us on television, we worry. When talk show hosts publicly introduce, even applaud, one lewd pathology after another, we worry. When obscene art is supported by tax dollars, and Hollywood is supported by politicians, we worry. When yesterday's decency is replaced by NC-17 movie ratings, earlier prime times, museums exhibiting pornography, federal agencies bowing to liberal courts, and role models whose gift to kids is perversion, we worry.

Is our concern justified? Or, is today's entertainment just a new art form, unique to this generation?

Jan and Richard

15 April

Dear Jan and Richard:

I share your concern over what is commonly referred to as entertainment. Whatever happened to movies like *Boy's Town*, *Going My Way*, *The Sound of Music*, or Frank Capra's, *It's A Wonderful Life*? These films were not only entertaining, but provided timeless values every family could learn from.

In *It's A Wonderful Life*, Jimmy Stewart and Donna Reed legitimized, "till death do us part" as they experienced one setback after another. Stewart's character, George Bailey, was taught that every person touches others, and that with true friends all adversity can be conquered. In the final scene George realizes that all of us have a guardian angel.

Fantasy? Old-fashioned? Or just sound principles for all to enjoy? In our day, Emmys were given to actors, actresses, and directors who did not ridicule family values. And the one and only TV talk show host told us, "Kids say the darndest things."

Raphael, Donahue, Rivera, and a host of newcomers, continually seek the bizarre, hoping to capture a larger share of the tabloid market. Their entertainment selections typically include: Transsexualism, Strip Clubs for Couples, Spousal Homicide, Lesbianism, Gay Couples With Children, and Sexual Misconduct of the Clergy.

The greater the freak show, the higher chance of airing. Hosts justify their programs as self-help for the 0.000001 percent of the population who are "victimized" by various disorders.

How about some positive family stories? Not a chance. In fact, two talk show producers told the author of a parenting book that interviews with successful parents and their children would be of no interest to viewers because "parents don't raise children like that anymore." Said another way, there's no sleaze, eccentric behavior, or current controversy offered by the likes of Sherrol Miller. According to the *Wall Street Journal*, Sherrol has appeared on three Donohue, two Raphael, one Geraldo, Rivers, and Montel Williams' shows. Ms. Miller's story was her marriage to a gay, con-man bigamist.

Ask people like Judge Thomas or O.J. Simpson if they enjoy the public attention their stories generate. Do they find their exploited lives entertaining?

Money talks. Ask Amy Fisher, the modern day "Lolita," who one day may be rich because networks trampled each other in a rush to produce another valueless travesty. The same thing happened when the O. J. story broke. The message to Hollywood agents: camp outside the latest prison riot, religious cult standoff, or public trial; get the story; the rights to the book or movie; the money.

Content is unimportant. What children might see or hear is irrelevant. All that matters is that advertisers will

buy, the public will watch, and the publisher will publish.
Anything that sells is entertaining, especially to those who
profit from immorality.

This pandering is not unique to Hollywood and the
networks. Radio stations sell their souls to buy the latest
"shock jock" whose obscene format keeps the FCC mail-
man employed. Book chains and libraries purchase worthless "sex" books under the guise of providing entertainment to readers. Record companies and MTV entertain
the young with words and images designed to satisfy hedonistic youth. And, as you suggest, museums offer an
entertainment package to old and young alike who are
willing to pay for a "Gamorah Gallery."

Your concerns are justified; your attention needed.
Don't accept the argument that this "entertainment" is
nothing more than a new art form. What is different is the
industry's willingness to abandon all sense of what is right—
regardless of how far out of touch they are with the American family.

Danika

---

15 April

Dear Jan and Richard:

Entertainment, like beauty, is in the eye of the beholder. With music, for example, generation after generation of kids disagreed with their parents about what did or
did not sound good. Moms and dads often freaked-out
over lyrics while children rocked 'n rolled to the beat,
oblivious to the message.

Talk show celebrities continue to hold onto ratings
because they courageously discuss topics which capture
the interest of viewers. Though many adults support your
position, they are still drawn to the program.

Why? Could it be that they are entertained? Are millions of Donahue viewers any different from car racing

fans who secretly hope for a crash? How about hockey fans who buy tickets to see the fights? Why do newspapers carry special "soap" columns? Isn't it to keep the faithful up to date on the latest affair, abortion, incest, wife beating, or child abuse incident?

Consider rock stars. Most baby boom parents cringe at the sights and sounds of artists who fill the entertainment needs of children. When these personalities fight for a clean environment, kids listen. When they wear red ribbons at award ceremonies, symbolizing their fight against AIDS, kids remember. When they give of their time to help raise money for the hungry, kids respond by attending concerts, buying music, and wearing their image—all because the customer was entertained.

Even controversial art exhibits draw crowds. Ironically, no one ever heard of Mapplethorpe or Serrano until the media planted the seed that their talents were different. No one cared about 2 Live Crew until a right-wing judge said their music was obscene. And, thanks to the press and the courts, more people were entertained.

Entertainment is like values. Only the individual can judge what is good or bad. The characters Snow White, Bambi, and The Little Mermaid had adversaries who claimed their stories were upsetting to children. *Snow White* involved witchcraft. The murder of Bambi's mother was too violent. The Little Mermaid disobeyed her father. Even so, millions of children and their parents were entertained.

What's the answer? Can Hollywood be held accountable for the taste of others? Can the networks refuse to air news segments demanded by the public? And, most important, can a free society be forbidden to read, see, or hear entertainment which some find inappropriate? The answer, of course, is NO.

The day we establish entertainment restrictions is the day our kids surrender their liberties. As parents and grandparents we must never allow such an indignity.

Darcee

                                                        18 April
Dear Darcee and Danika:

It seems that the entertainment issue is subject to those
who decide what the public wants, or, what they want to
give the public. If, as you stated, Darcee, "Entertainment,
like beauty, is in the eye of the beholder," then all of us
are at the mercy of those who decide what is, and what is
not, entertainment.

If Hollywood, the media, and TV's elite have different
attitudes on social issues, then their morals will determine
which images and messages children experience.

In his book, *The Home Invaders*, Donald Wildmon
stressed this point, citing the Lichter and Rothmann Study.
Hour-long interviews were conducted with 240 journalists
and broadcasters from the *New York Times*, the *Washington
Post*, the *Wall Street Journal*, *Time* magazine, *Newsweek*, *U.S.
News & World Report*, and the news departments at CBS,
NBC, ABC, PBS. Also interviewed were 104 of "television's
creative community" including 15 presidents of independent production companies, 18 executive producers (26 of
whom were also writers), and 10 network vice presidents
responsible for program development and selection. The
following chart reflects entertainment industry and news
representatives' attitudes.

Attitude On Social Issues	News TV	Movie	Media Elite
(% agreeing with statement)			
Woman has right to decide			
on abortion	90%	97%	96%
Strongly agree adultery is wrong	15%	16%	13%
Seldom or never attend worship	86%	93%	96%

We believe that in the vast majority of cities, towns, and
rural communities, no research team would ever find a 90
percent plus pro-abortion vote, nor would only 13 percent
to 16 percent of the adult population "strongly agree adul-

tery is wrong," and certainly far more citizens actively worship than do the study's respondents.

This attitude difference concerns us. Is the entertainment industry reflective of society, or molding society?

Jan and Richard

---

21 April

Dear Jan and Richard:

I'll say it again. Entertainers continue to succeed because they satisfy the public's need. Do you think advertisers would underwrite production costs for talk shows if the host and guests didn't draw a large enough audience? Do you think Hollywood executives would invest millions of dollars in movies that wouldn't make a profit? And, do you honestly believe network news stories are planted in favor of a particular social agenda? The public wouldn't stand for it.

When Andres Serrano produced the photo of a crucifix submerged in his own urine, no one much cared until it was learned that he received a $10,000 grant from the National Endowment for the Arts. Lawmakers screamed and much of the public was outraged. Yet, the media carried the story, not to support Serrano's action, but to report the event.

The movie *Basic Instinct* was advertised as a murder mystery with plenty of sex scenes. Moviegoers flocked to see the film. No one paid their admission ticket for them. And, you can bet many of those moviegoers also patronize their local church.

Though Danika's letter objected to the "talk show tabloid," she failed to explain why the hosts continue to dominate their time slot ratings day after day, year after year.

Danika also overlooks reality. How many adolescents do you know would pay to see a movie with all the excitement of a 1950's Dracula? Would kids of divorce enjoy the Jimmy Stewart, Donna Reed love story? And, though the Judge Thomas hearings were explicit, isn't there benefit

in assuring our youth that the selection of a Supreme
Court Justice is serious business?

Children have a right to learn. If that means holding
their attention through graphic messages or high-tech
images, then so be it. In either case, the kids will decide
what is and what is not entertainment—just like you did
when you were young.

If you think about it, how many of your children's
entertainment habits did you abhor? Was it their music?
Movies? Woodstock? Anti-establishment speeches? Did you
find their desire to grow up unsettling? What's changed?

Well, for one thing, your kids are now the loving parents of your grandchildren. And even though your tastes
differed from your son's and daughter's, you continue to
love your children—the same kids whose youthful rebellion was magnified by their entertainment choices.

Were they brainwashed? Were you, when you were
young? Of course not. Nor are today's youth under the
spell of Hollywood personalities, sport heroes, or rock
music stars.

In fact, the only real danger parents and grandparents
face comes from doomsday prophets who are intimidated
by a progressive industry whose only business is pleasure.

Though both of you may find the Lichter & Rothmann
study unsettling, keep in mind that every respondent in
that survey is successful. And isn't success what we really
want for our children and grandchildren?

                                                    Darcee

---

                              21 April

Dear Jan & Richard:

It's no mistake that Hollywood packages adultery as
an exciting alternative to marriage. The media's biased
pro-abortion coverage is well documented. And, not sur-
prisingly, religion is continuously mocked in network specials, TV dramas, and Hollywood movies.

Is it just the L.A. rat race that has driven thousands of families to relocate, or could declining morals play a part? Why do beautiful San Francisco and culturally rich New York City both earn the "nice place to visit, but I wouldn't want to live there" label?

Maybe the answer is tolerance—the kind of tolerance that promotes homosexuality, promiscuity, adultery, and secularism; the kind that hides behind the First Amendment, regardless of the consequences to the family.

Darcee admonishes you for not recognizing that Hollywood and media executives are successful. Is success measured by what someone owns or gives? Should we accept materialistic and name-recognition indicators as criteria for success? Must we legitimize their products as entertainment. No! If we analyze their works for redeeming values, we are sure to condemn the entertainers contribution to society.

Consider the Romans. They didn't initially burn Christians. First, they pitted them against gladiators for public entertainment. Some were spared. But, as the thirst for violence grew, more Christians died. Torturing Christians progressed to feeding them to wild animals. Roman entertainment soon became a circus of horrors.

Desensitization can be found throughout the entertainment industry. Murder is graphic. Sex is explicit. Language is vulgar. Young and old alike accept lower and lower standards of decency. Children assure parents that they hear it on the bus. Producers rationalize their support of immoral programming as the industry's right to free expression. News anchors justify "live and in-color" as being responsive to the viewer's right to know. Meanwhile, parents try their best to protect their children's innocence.

Entertainment is often a diversion. The process can be subtle, even subliminal. Mesmerization of audiences by news and entertainment personalities results in moral decay. Moses discovered similar consequences upon his descent from God's holy mountain. No sooner had he left, the liberated Israelites decided to engage in debauchery.

The people traded God's law for a golden idol. The result was disaster.

The day parents surrender to the desires of the entertainment industry will be the day children submit to an immoral world. We must never let this happen.

Danika

Part II
Reverse Role Models

. . . the antihero has nothing to worship but himself and his art, and is inescapably tugged down to the temporal, the mundane and the dark. The hero seeks not happiness but goodness, and his fulfillment lies in achieving it. . . . His example tells us that we fail, not by aiming too high in life, but by aiming far too low.

—Dr. George Roche
A World Without Heroes

21 April

Dear Darcee and Danika:

It's tough being a single dad. You not only have to play the mother/father role, but you're also expected to be your child's hero. Though my seven-year-old son and four-year-old daughter still see me as the role model I wish to project, the day will come when other heroes will enter their lives.

What concerns me is the number of kids who seem to worship what I would call "plastic idols." Rock, screen, and sports celebrities vie for the purchasing power and adulation of children.

How can parents guard against inappropriate hero worship? Who can we safely use as role models? What role should parents play in determining who is, and who is not, a positive influence?

Gillie

24 April

Dear Gillie:

Hero worship has always been a societal phenomenon. Too often, heroes are created by the media. When U.S. soldiers went to Somalia to feed the starving, many people stated that our military was a shining example of heroism. In fact, *U.S. News & World Report* reported that "through Dec. 1, 1992, 'Somalia' was mentioned 2,300 times in major newspapers. Madonna was mentioned 4,300 times."

From the time children are old enough to turn on the TV, media heroes begin to make an impact. Unfortunately, instead of learning about "Honest Abe," the kids are mesmerized by the likes of Rambo, Freddie Krueger, and multi-millionaire sports personalities.

In adolescent years, kids are drawn to the "90210—Beverly Hills" gang. When teenagers mature, Donald Trump-type role models fulfill fantasies for quick-buck pleasure-seeking youth.

Even Hollywood is confused. In the original movie *Cape Fear* Gregory Peck was a devoted family man. His 1990's successor, Nick Nolte is a philanderer. Meanwhile, Jesus of Nazareth is portrayed as a confused Messiah in *The Last Temptation of Christ*.

Other heroes have fallen from grace. For five hundred years Christopher Columbus was regarded as the man who discovered America, but is now suspect for bringing disease and death to peace loving native Americans.

The media pursues "stories from the stars," such as Ice-T with his "Cop Killer" recording, yet not one reporter covered the story of a memorial dedicated to ten thousand police officers who were killed in the line of duty. Children's action heroes have also taken a turn for the worse. At one time, fictional characters like Superman were too busy fighting evil to be bothered by sexual fantasies, or nude photography. Yet, the comic book industry has done its part to humanize yesteryear's role models.

Marvel Comics even created a gay superhero who fights homophobia and AIDS discrimination.

Real heroism is declining. The Mayor of Los Angeles celebrated Freddie Krueger Day. A movie producer wants to portray the Marion Barry (convicted Mayor of Washington, D.C.) story. Sinead O'Connor ripped up a picture of Pope John Paul II and then was defended by Hollywood for exercising her freedom of speech.

What can parents do? First, recognize that moms and dads are their children's heroes. Setting a positive example for children is the primary objective. Second, point out the differences between false and real heroes. Emphasize the policeman who prevents a teenager from committing suicide, the fireman who rushes into the burning house to save a child, the teacher whose love for kids is reflected in his or her students' performance, or clergy who minister to the poor, the lonely, the dying. Conversely, expose the shallowness of athletes who refuse to sign a young fan's autograph book, while negotiating for higher salaries, paid for by that same fan's ticket. Call attention to news reporters who dote on mega-star sexual habits, overlooking their promiscuous behavior. And above all, never let the media hero's $1,000 contribution to the poor be misconstrued as charity. You and I both know a $1,000 donation is a small sacrifice compared to the biblical woman who dropped but a single coin in the collection box.

Third, use history to illustrate the values associated with past heroes. George Washington is remembered for his courage; Abe Lincoln for standing by his convictions; Jesus, His compassion.

When others enter into and influence your children's lives, be sure your kids are aware of your approval rating. Only then can a parent be confident of those other heroes.

Danika

24 April

Dear Gillie:

In a national poll junior high and high school students rated their heroes. Neither parents nor religious leaders registered even 1 percent. Of note, actors, musicians, comedians, and sports stars all found favor with the kids.

At first glance, parents should be alarmed, yet, doesn't hero worship come with adolescence? Isn't it realistic to expect even the youngest of our citizens to latch onto superheroes, or teens to swoon to every word, action, or picture of their favorite celebrity? What's new? Nothing! Didn't your mom fall in love with Rhett Butler when he saved Scarlett from certain death? How about your father, didn't he approve of General Eisenhower's leadership during the invasion of France? And what about your generation? Weren't the Beatles, Elvis and others, all eligible for hero worship?

If you answered yes to any of these questions, then how can you and your colleagues spend precious parenting time worrying about whom your children identify as heroes? Today's hero is tomorrow's memory. If it were not so, then the Mutant Turtles poster would still be on your teenager's wall. Interests change; so will your child's heroes.

Your second question, "Which role models can we safely use as examples?" is interesting. Imagine trying to convince your teenager that Paula Abdul and Sandi Patti both have a nice message, or telling your son that he really would enjoy the movie, *A River Runs Through It*. Your kids would wonder if you had "flipped out," much the same way you wondered about your mom and dad who questioned your taste in entertainment.

Addressing your third issue—the role parents play in hero selection—I believe parents must play a part, not as judge and jury, but as facilitators. Ask your kids what they like best about their favorite rock, movie, or sports star.

Help them understand why qualities like racial tolerance, respect for the environment, and compassion for those with AIDS, all represent favorable hero characteristics. Point out that negative press about celebrities is often fictionalized, especially by those who have a personal agenda—like limiting freedom of speech.

Occasionally, you may disagree with your child's hero. But remember, if you attempt to force your opinion on your children, you run the risk of rebellion. Better to wait out the storm. Besides, you may discover that someone you thought was a poor role model, may well turn out to be a shining example for your son or daughter to emulate.

Gillie, I began this letter by pointing out that parents didn't fare well in a recent poll. Don't be alarmed. As parents you really don't want to be the only heroes your children know, any more than you want to be your child's only friend.

Heroes are for kids. Let them choose their idols.

                                                                Darcee

---

                                27 April

Dear Danika and Darcee:

It's interesting that while Danika recommends active parental participation in monitoring children's role models, Darcee seems to favor a more passive approach, allowing kids to learn from experience.

Isn't there a middle road parents can take? Danika, shouldn't we encourage kids to find positive qualities in celebrities, even if their behavior may at times be questionable? And what about Darcee's point, that heroes will "come and go" as children mature?

Darcee, if parents' concern over hero worship is blown out of proportion, then why are there so many studies and commentaries about the lack of real heroes in our society? Isn't there a direct correlation between the lack of heroes and the decline in morals?

                                                                Gillie

30 April

Dear Gillie:

Be careful of "middle road" parenting. The inference is too close to moral relativity—where there is no right, no wrong, only whatever feels good. And that's the problem with too many music, movie, TV, and sports personalities.

Though Darcee's "this too will pass" philosophy is tempting, parents must realize that early values impressed on kids will likely stay with them through maturity. If this were not true, then why should parents waste time giving their children a moral foundation?

As for finding positives in all celebrities, let's weigh the implications. Even the most obnoxious human being can display a good side. Yet, one must wonder why some rock singers who have young children publicly denounce the lyrics they sell to other kids. Isn't that ironic? When Magic Johnson criticizes the government's AIDS research commitment, yet fails to condemn immoral behavior, isn't the message inconsistent?

When you were growing up in the sixties, youth was synonymous with rebellion. Vietnam and everyone associated with that calamity incurred the wrath of our nation's young people. Why? Was it lack of trust? Were not our nation's politicians and military leaders inconsistent in word and deed?

When Spiro Agnew was a Republican candidate for Vice President, he proudly proclaimed, "A Nixon-Agnew Administration will abolish the credibility gap and reestablish the truth, the whole truth, as its policy." Meanwhile, the nation's top military commander in Vietnam continued to mislead the public with one rosy forecast after another. In 1964 General Westmoreland began a series of inaccurate predictions about the war. In April of that year he stated, "It is inconceivable that the Viet Cong could ever defeat the Armed Forces of South Vietnam." Three years later the General announced, "The military picture is favorable." In early 1968, General Westmoreland proudly proclaimed, "The enemy is about to run out of steam." Four years later, and now Chief of Staff of the U.S. Army, he was quoted in the *Washington Star* as stating, "We're on our way up . . . the pendulum is beginning to swing." The rest is history.

If the sixties generation couldn't trust, and, in many cases for good reason, the leaders of the country, why would they blindly trust the likes of Axl Rose, Magic Johnson, Madonna, and a host of others whose immorality represents a new lie? The sixties kids are today's parents. They should know better.

These nurturers of youth should be suspicious when Hollywood shows police in a negative light three times out of every four. Parents should question why Hollywood no longer portrays role models like *Boy's Town's* Father Flanagan, or Bing Crosby's character, Father O'Mally. Parents should also be skeptical of athletes who have traded love of the game for love of money.

Heroes, real or otherwise, will come and go. But their deeds will remain. Remember the Wicked Witch who said, "I'll get you my pretty, and your little dog too!"

Danika

---

30 April

Dear Gillie:

It's amazing how often we hear about our nation's moral decline. As your letter infers, there must be a relationship between this decay and the never-ending stories and gossip about immoral role models. Let's put rumors to rest.

America is the richest country in the world, representing the world's ideal of freedom. Tens of thousands of refugees cross our borders to live the American dream. Even with immorality on the increase, or so the critics say, we still have the guts to fight evil on foreign shores, while reaching in our pockets to feed the Third World.

Everywhere we turn there's heroism. From ABC's "Person of the Week" to Washington's "Points of Light," we find examples of people who have helped others.

Athletes donate their autographs to help fund raisers. Rock stars donate their talents to raise money for worthwhile causes. Movie stars campaign to protect the environment. TV personalities appear on this "thon" and that "thon" because they want to help. Look at AIDS benefits. Celebrities proudly parade before cameras telling the public we must all do what we can to eradicate this horrible disease. Without their voices, many will die. Without their witnessing, many young people would never understand why we must win the war against AIDS.

Heroes are people. People are human. And humans make mistakes. Pete Rose—arrested for gambling—said, "My father taught me that the only way you can make good at anything is to practice and then practice some more." Woody Hayes—fired for improper sideline behavior—said, "In picking an assistant coach, the first thing I was interested in was the man's character." John McEnroe—accused of irrational courtside behavior—said, "I just can't be what you call a crowd pleaser. I have to be me." Magic Johnson—retired because of AIDS: "Even when I went to the playground, I never picked the best players. I picked guys with less talent, but who were willing to work hard, who had the desire to be great." John F. Kennedy, accused womanizer, said, "Being courageous requires no exceptional qualifications, no magic formula, no special combination of time, place and circumstances. It is an opportunity that sooner or later is presented to us all."

All of these people were role models. And, for thousands of kids, they were heroes. So who are we to challenge the status bestowed by our children on today's motivators? Is it right to cast the first stone? No sooner will we chastise our teenagers' rock star than we learn that their idol has a special ranch for handicapped children. Who then will look the fool?

"I am not concerned that you have fallen; I am concerned that you arise." These words were spoken by Abraham Lincoln. Let's never forget them.

Darcee

Part III
Freedom of Speech and Other Incantations

The whole philosophy of our country has changed to accept immorality, degeneracy, pornographic movies. I'm the world's greatest advocate of the First Amendment, but somehow we've got to have freedom with some responsibility.

—Benjamin Hooks
Past Executive Director
NAACP

---

30 April

Dear Darcee and Danika:

John and I are firm believers in "freedom of speech." Since we are somewhat younger parents we may even be classified as liberal by our parents' standards. But, as parents of young children, we can't help but wonder where free speech advocates draw the line when it comes to protecting kids from immorality.

Please provide your insight on how far you feel the "freedom train" will travel.

John and Ronica

---

2 May

Dear John & Ronica:

Rarely will freedom of speech advocates sacrifice their right in order to protect children from immorality. Their argument goes something like this. "If you force libraries to prohibit children from checking out R-rated videos, you are in fact forcing censorship down the throats of all of us. Where will the demand stop? Next, you'll demand that we burn books you don't like!" Those who make such radical arguments fail to ask whether children are harmed when society fails to protect them from the prurient interests of adults.

In 1939, Hollywood broke the cursing barrier when Rhett uttered, "Frankly my dear, I don't give a damn." Much of the public was outraged. Interestingly, the movies produced in the forties, many of which were "blood and guts" war stories, contained no cursing.

But, this restraint was not to continue. The 1990 movie *Goodfellas* used the "F" word almost three hundred times. Hollywood didn't mind, as the Motion Picture Academy nominated the movie for an Oscar.

The movie industry even produced a new rating (NC-17) to remove the "X" stigma. This strategy backfired at the box office. Movie producers had to tone down pornographic scenes to avoid loss of adolescent ticket sales, causing artists and producers to scream censorship.

The recording industry is often more adamant in their demands to protect *your* rights. The group 2 Live Crew remains "As Nasty As They Wanna Be," while Ice-T encourages youth to blow away cops.

In a related trade, radio talk show hosts spew almost anything from their microphones. No wonder some hosts are called "shock jocks." Their X-rated homilies cover everything from lesbian sexual habits, to discussions on the pros and cons of a mother's right to have a baby who may inherit a genetic deformity. Sensationalism sells. The public has a need to know. We shouldn't tamper with the First Amendment. Garbage!

Though the "freedom train" has gone too far, the public can still choose decency over the gutter. Not so with the National Endowment for the Arts. This government agency funnels tax dollars to subsidize "artists" like Mapplethorpe who photographed little girls with their vaginas exposed. Another "artist" received an NEA grant for photographing a crucifix in a glass of his own urine!

This is art? It's freedom of expression according to the NEA—the same agency that rejected sculptures which now adorn Washington's National Cathedral.

Something's wrong when freedom overrides morality. And, unless parents stop this "runaway train," there will be many casualties among our youth.

Danika

---

2 May

Dear John & Ronica:

Freedom of speech is the very heart of this great nation. The right to say what we believe is nowhere more profound than in the news and entertainment industries. From Hollywood to New York, media personalities are taking a leadership role in the fight for social justice, cultural diversity, and the protection of the environment. And some of these artists have dramatically demonstrated their convictions by challenging heretofore untouchable institutions for their crimes against humanity.

Were it not for vocalist Sinead O'Connor's courage, the public may have forgotten the injustices perpetrated by the Roman Catholic Church. If rapper Ice-T and activist Sister Souljah had ignored racism and police brutality, where would the public's conscience be? If CBS had chosen to cancel "Picket Fences" storylines about fetal tissue research, AIDS discrimination, the dangers of teaching sexual abstinence, and intolerance for those with differing orientations, these issues may have never been exposed.

Freedom of speech issues are not the sole domain of celebrities. Consider parents who choose to sue the Boy Scouts rather than force their atheist children to submit to a religious oath; or the father who took his daughter's case to the Supreme Court when she was humiliated by a graduation commencement speech that endorsed religion. The freedom of speech defense is not only a justifiable argument for enlightening the public, but it also protects citizens from the evils of censorship.

Hitler, Stalin and Chairman Mao all understood the power of censorship. Unfortunately, millions of people died at the hands of their power. Hitler said, "If I can control the textbooks, I can control Germany." The same could be said about music, movies, art, and other forms of entertainment.

Who's to say that today's "bizarre" images may not in fact become the twenty-first century's standard of decency? When Elvis swiveled his hips, parents were embarrassed. When the Beatles shook their long hair, parents were disgusted. When Woodstock presented images of nudity, drinking and drugs, parents were mortified. Still, the same kids who shocked their parents are now loving parents themselves.

Jerry Kirk, President of The National Coalition For The Protection of Children & Families, stated, "If Americans know what obscenity is, and know that the key to law enforcement is contemporary community standards, and know that those standards are established by citizens, they will rise up en masse." So why hasn't this happened? Could it be that obscenity cannot be defined. Is the problem freedom of choice? If music, movie, art, etc., is indeed immoral, then why does it sell? Even the Supreme Court has trouble defining what is morally acceptable.

Freedom of speech is not only for liberals. If it were, basketball stars, like A.C. Green of the Los Angeles Lakers, wouldn't be featured as a twenty-nine-year-old virgin. When religious athletes, musicians, or Hollywood personalities "thank God" for their success on national TV, haven't they exercised their rights? Isn't their message good for your children's ears? Do the networks complain? No. Artists? No. Record companies? No. The press? No. Why? Because freedom of speech is a liberty worth defending, regardless of content.

How far will the "freedom train" travel? Far away from right-wing fundamentalists whose only objective is to derail your children's right to free speech—free expression and freedom of choice.

Darcee

5 May

Dear Darcee and Danika:

Freedom of speech seems to fire up passions on both sides. All one has to do is read your letters to understand how really far apart both of you are on this issue.

After sharing your opinions with the Parents' Association, we decided to ask one question. Is there ever a time when parents should deny children their constitutional right to freedom of speech, and its cousin, freedom of expression?

John and Ronica

---

8 May

Dear John and Ronica:

The only time parents have the right to withhold their child's constitutional privileges is if the child is too young to differentiate between fiction and reality, or cannot understand language or visuals used. To deny literally means to refuse or reject. Parents must ask, "Are we denying our kids' freedom of speech and/or expression because we refuse to accept the validity of this right for children, or because we refuse to accept the content or action associated with the messenger's desire to express themselves?"

If the former, parents are wrong. If the latter, such actions may be understandable. For instance, if parents conform to laws forbidding movie patrons to yell "fire" in a theatre, because such action could result in injury, then parents are well within their bounds to restrain their children.

If parents are offended by a T-shirt imprinted with "just do it" and prohibit their child from wearing it, that may well be an infringement of the child's First Amendment freedoms. Conflicts are especially likely when adults misconstrue "just do it" as encouraging sexual activity. The Nike Company, which created the slogan, sees the message as a positive motivational phrase which challenges children to do their best.

Parents have the right to restrain their young children from cursing, viewing R-rated movies, watching MTV videos and the like. But once kids are old enough to understand the message, parents should back off. Instead of denying kids these experiences, parents should explain what they believe is offensive. Parents may still demonstrate freedom of choice by turning off the TV, boycotting an art show, or by not purchasing a product inappropriate for young children.

Before I leave this topic, allow me to share my opinions about Danika's May second letter. First, Danika's appeal for protecting children from the "prurient interests of adults" is, at best, a weak argument. Better that one child watch an R-rated film than to force censorship down the throats of all of us. Second, Danika uses two NEA artists out of thousands whose excellent work is funded by the federal government.

Finally, parents must teach tolerance by setting an example themselves. If parents are intolerant of their children's freedoms, how will these kids raise their own children? How will the young learn to discern if their parents prohibit them from experiencing freedom of speech and expression? Don't deny your kids their rights. Deny them exposure to other parents who would censor childhood.

Darcee

---

8 May

Dear John and Ronica:

There will be many times when parents must disappoint their children; when mom and dad say "no"; when discipline is necessary; when other family members have a greater need; and when the adult must do what's best for the child, regardless of peer pressure, invasion of privacy, and so-called children's rights.

Because of this nation's "freedom-at-any-cost" mentality, the family has been imprisoned by immorality. Parents
dare not turn their backs on TV; children aren't allowed
to walk to the corner store; adolescents are continually
hoodwinked by advertising fads; and teenagers are pres-
sured to exchange virtue for experience.

When claiming rights, one must remember the word
"responsibility." Parents are responsible for raising their
children. It is the mother's and father's right to teach what
they believe is appropriate. If their authority is in conflict
with the freedom demands of their kids, so be it. Be accountable. Do not acquiesce to immoral behavior. The
children will one day thank you for exercising your prerogative.

In answer to your question, "Is there ever a time when
parents should deny children their constitutional right to
freedom of speech and it's cousin, freedom of expression?" The answer is yes. Whenever your moral code is
challenged by man-made laws and freedoms, a higher law
must prevail. Only then will the family avoid anarchy.

On a related subject, I would like to make a few obser-
vations about Darcee's position on freedom. First, the
"heart" of this great nation began pumping when God-
fearing men and women brought Judeo-Christian morality to America. Is it any wonder that the phrase "turn over
in their grave" often refers to Bill of Rights' authors.

Whatever happened to democracy? Is Darcee suggest-
ing that celebrities who champion causes for the (very)
few, be allowed to demean the values of the vast majority?
When a father is allowed to disrupt a nation's religious
history because his daughter was offended, society is weakened. And, if nothing is to be censored, then why not cast
off our clothes, have sex with animals and teach our children freedom of perversion? Where will it end?

Darcee's question as to why the vast majority of the
public is silent, is a good one. Are we too busy? Apathetic?
Unsure of what must be done? Or, is complacency the
freedom train's fuel? Do we really believe that the lifestyle

we give our children will insulate them from continued decline in public morals?

Meanwhile, parents can only question why their honor-role son was beaten up at a rock concert; the retarded girl raped by a football team is too confused to understand; children kidnapped and murdered by other kids will never hear the reasons why their lives were so worthless; and as five-year-old boys question the meaning of oral sex, their seven-year-old sisters are introduced to the world of lesbianism. Freedoms rage on. Where will it end?

It isn't right-wing fundamentalists you must fear. It's conservatives, liberals, moderates, and other "enlightened" adults who have fallen asleep at the parenting wheel.

Danika

Part IV
Shock Theatre

What scares and appalls me, Dr. Dobson, is when I see what's on cable TV, some of the movies . . . that come into homes today, is stuff that they wouldn't show in X-rated adult theaters thirty years ago . . . as it gets into the home to the children who may be unattended or unaware that they may be a Ted Bundy.
—Ted Bundy interview with
Dr. James Dobson, hours before his execution.

8 May

Dear Darcee and Danika:

We just received a notice from the American Family Association announcing that Phil Donahue would like to show a live execution on his TV show. Yesterday we heard the lyrics from a Guns "n" Roses album promoting racism and violence. And tonight our favorite family TV show introduced condoms as alternatives to sexual abstinence.

Does anyone care that childhood may soon be extinct? Is it really necessary to show it all or say it all? Will "shock theatre," with its violent and sexually explicit material, result in the manufacture of future Ted Bundy's?

Brina and Hasheem

---

11 May

Dear Brina and Hasheem:

When Phil Donahue came to television, his bold format was praised by critics across the country for having the courage to tackle real issues. Thanks to his vision and that of his colleagues, America now has a better understanding of, and appreciation for, the problems which plague our country.

Homosexuality, sexual harassment, teen prostitution and child pornography are real, as is wife beating, incest, priest pedophilia, etc. So why hide the truth? Do you think today's societal ills are a product of the nineties?

Let's look at your initial objection—a live execution. If you asked a random sample of citizens what their number one fear is, they likely would say, "violent crime." And Donahue would agree. In fact, when questioned about his proposed TV execution he was quoted as saying, "What's wrong with it? Let's see future bad guys watch these people fry right here on television." And maybe violent criminals may sit up and take notice, while violent youth would get the message.

I can use the same argument to justify producers' decisions to air segments about the increasing tendency among Catholic priests to sexually abuse children. Without the victim's testimony and "disguised" interviews with the perpetrator, children remain at risk.

The same service is provided by victims of rapists, wife beaters, and any number of the sexually harassed who tell their story. Donahue has exposed those who prey on society; for such courage, we should be grateful.

Turning to another medium, rock music represents to youth what TV talk shows represent to parents—a way to experience reality. Ice-T, Guns "n" Roses, and other popular idols package societal ills in a way that young people can understand.

Racism, harassment, and bigotry are fairly represented in lyric and video. These mediums are just other forms of education.

When a rock star's ballad cries out for condom protection against AIDS, public awareness of police brutality, or a teenager's rights, our youth are being served. Interestingly, parents who condemn these stars and their messages refuse to educate their children about these vital issues.

TV and rock music industries are criticized by the religious right as marketers of graphic violence and sensationalized sex. The truth is, kids will not turn on, or tune in to "Lawrence Welk," "Mr. Rogers," or "Little House on the Prairie." They will turn on to truth—especially when visually stimulating. They will respond to messages which challenge the establishment. As products of the sixties you both understand this.

Violent and sexually explicit material will not give birth to future Ted Bundys. But, failure to educate youth on the realities of such behaviors may well result in an increase in victims of such pathological behavior.

Darcee

---

11 May

Dear Brina and Hasheem:

It's hard to believe that anyone could argue that violent and sexually explicit material has little effect on childhood. Look at the facts. More than one thousand studies in the last thirty years have made the correlation between violent entertainment and aggressive and antisocial behavior. One major study from the National Institute of Mental Health leaves little doubt that a steady diet of TV violence can have adverse effects on viewers. Further, heavy

doses of TV viewing can negatively impact academic performance, as the tube replaces both schoolwork and pas-
time reading.

Television has become the leading sex educator. In
the last ten years soap opera sexual content has increased
more than 100 percent. Meanwhile, talk show hosts parade every sexual disorder imaginable on TV screens across
America. Music videos add to the educational process with
their suggestive vignettes, while beer bimbos promise unlimited pleasures for "real men" who drink the sponsor's
product.

Researchers estimate that the average sixteen year old
will watch 15,000 sexual acts on TV annually. And, it's
estimated that by age sixteen kids will have seen 200,000
portrayals of TV violence, including 33,000 murders.

Still, networks continue to deny any culpability for
youth violence. This same industry says TV has little impact on viewer behavior, yet they gladly cash in on the
billions of advertising dollars received from products promoted to the public. This may lead one to ask: "Why
bother with 'Say no to drugs' commercials if they have no
effect on youth?"

In one TV study there was a 160 percent rise in incidents of hitting, kicking and biting among first and second graders. Interestingly, of eighty-five major studies on
TV violence and aggression in children, only one report
denied any relationship. That study was commissioned by
NBC.

In the spring of '91 prime time shows promoting sexual
activity outside marriage were thirteen times more common than shows supporting marital sex. Is it any wonder
that a national poll that same year found only 3 percent
of Americans felt TV portrayed "very positive values."

Does Hollywood care about childhood? Does MTV
weigh the impact of sexually explicit rock videos on youth?
Do major networks and cable monopolies worry about the
long-term effect violence has on children? Do musicians
cringe when pre-adolescent youth attend their concerts?

Do Donahue, Jones, Raphael and the rest of the talk show gang worry about the latchkey child who is drawn to their afternoon freak shows? The answer to these questions is a resounding NO! Should society have worried about Ted Bundy when his addiction to pornography began to intensify? Yes! Should society worry that among our youth there may well exist a future Bundy, Dahmer, or Gayce? Yes again!

We had better worry. But, more important, we'd better be willing to stop the liquidation of childhood.

Danika

---

14 May

Dear Darcee and Danika:

Darcee, your view that "anything goes" is troubling. Could it be that our kids are at risk because our nation has gone too far in exposing them to situations before they are ready? Please read Danika's letter. We need convincing that your position will not result in more Ted Bundys.

Danika, Darcee does appear to make a valid point when she reminds parents that kids respond to music and rock stars whose message is intended to shock and get their attention. Can such content really impact kids whose home life is considered normal?

Brina and Hasheem

---

17 May

Dear Brina and Hasheem:

Poll after poll indicates that parents have little influence on their kids. This is a primary reason why television and Hollywood network executives recognize the awesome responsibility for providing quality programming.

To demonstrate this commitment, consider the number of Hollywood made-for-television specials produced to educate the public on current social issues. AIDS, wife beating, racism, child molestation, and homosexuality, to name a few, are classic examples of responsible programming.

Television talk show hosts tackle controversial topics other mediums avoid. The Spur Posse gang, teenage boys who kept score of their female conquests, was covered by no fewer than three shows. The issue was morality. Ten years ago this story would have been shunned by network television and the media. Today, thanks to the courage of talk show hosts, viewers are exposed to societal problems which affect us all. Airing controversy is only one public benefit. Entertainment is the other.

When "Married With Children," "Roseanne," or the "Simpsons" is aired, right-wing Christian activists "act up." The story line is bad, they say. The values are inappropriate, the language, the violence, the sex—that's the point. Ask most young people and they will tell you that *Total Recall* with all its violence, *Goodfellas* with all its vulgarity, *Basic Instinct* with all its sex, and *Silence of the Lambs* with all its horror, are merely entertaining. Soap operas feature beautiful people with ugly problems. Nothing more, nothing less. Talk show guests merely want to tell their stories while rock and rap lyrics are just words put to music. Even pornography is just another art form.

Parents would do well to recognize that the year 2000, not 1950, is around the corner.

Regarding Danika's letter, I am reminded of respected Hollywood producer, Rob Reiner, of "All In The Family," who warned that "sanctimonious Christians twist morality around when promoting values." And that's exactly the position Danika hides behind when she sells guilt to parents.

Don't fall for the lie. If all of society's ills are a direct result of the entertainment industry, then why is the product in such demand? Why has the government not stepped in to protect its citizens? Why do so many self-righteous preachers use the same medium to sell their message?

And, why would so many reputable companies support programming that would destroy its customers?

Until Danika can answer these questions, I would worry less about future Ted Bundys and more about individuals who would steal your children's rights.

Darcee

---

17 May

Dear Brina and Hasheem:

I agree with Darcee when she says that words, music and graphic violence can hold kids' attention. But, I disagree that such teasers are nothing more than entertainment.

Ice-T, the rapper who produced the "Cop Killer" album, created quite a stir when his lyrics suggested that police be murdered. It's "only words," Darcee would say. Yet, as Dr. James Dobson reported in his "Focus On The Family" monthly newsletter, Mr. Ice-T told Stanford University law students that the Los Angeles riot was "the happiest day of my life." Dobson reminds us that the riot resulted in 53 deaths, 2,400 injuries, 1,400 stores looted and burned, and more than $1 billion in property damage.

Alarming music lyrics come from a variety of entertainers. Satanism, racism, suicide, violence, drug and alcohol abuse, and sexual exploitation all have their mouthpieces. Consider the following messages from some of today's artists.

"A sacrifice, oh so nice, sacrifice to Lucifer, my master. Bring the chalice, raise the knife, welcome to my sacrifice."—Venom.

"Lovin every second, trying to make me blush, and all in all it was for the lust. I thought she was an angel and soft until I seen her come out with the whip and handcuffs."—Vanilla Ice.

"Broken splintered bones, boiling blood, torn and bleeding skin, blackened burning flesh, melting fat, amputated limbs, lungs torn out, heart ripped from the chest, decapitated, a meal of vaginas and breasts."—Predator

"Police and niggers, that's right, get outta my way. Don't need to buy none of your gold chains today. . . . Immigrants and faggots, they make no sense to me. They come to our country and think they'll do as they please. . . . Like start some mini-Iran or spread some f—— — disease."—Guns 'n' Roses

"Undress until your naked and put on this white coat. Now crush it, crush the cross. Suck the blood from this unholy life. Say after me, my soul belongs to Satan. Now you're into my coven, you are Lucifer's child."—King Diamond

"Breaking laws, knocking doors, but there's no one home. Made your bed, rest your head, but you lie there and moan. Where to hide, suicide is the only way out. Don't you know what it's really about?"—Ozzie Osbourne

"Ya get nothing for nothing, if that's what you do. Turn around b——, I've got use for you. Besides, you ain't got nothing better to do and I'm bored."—Guns 'n' Roses

"Not a woman, but a whore. I can taste the hate. Well, now I'm killing you . . . watch your face turning blue."— Motley Crue

"I smoke cheba, it helps me with my brain. I might be a little dusted but I'm not insane. . . . They'll be kicking out windows high on cocaine. . . . Policeman told my homeboy, 'put that crack out. You know you light up when the lights go down.' "—The Beastie Boys

"I've got my 12-guage sawed off. I got my headlights turned off. I'm 'bout to dust some shots off. I'm 'bout to dust some cops off."—Ice-T

". . . don't ever sleep, I'll wake you up with an axe. . . . I'll leave your bullet riddled body on the curb." — LL Cool J

"You can smoke a pound of bud (marijuana) everyday . . . that's the American dream."—Snoop Doggy Dogg

Another charming group is The Dead Kennedys. As if their group name isn't sickening enough, their lyrics from the song "I Kill Children" says it all. "I kill children and I love to see them die, I kill children, I make their mothers cry."

A popular band which goes by the acronym W.A.S.P. does not represent the Protestant work ethic. Rather, W.A.S.P. stands for: "We Are Sexual Perverts." And in California, the world's youngest punk rock band, Old Skull, originally sold more than 20,000 copies of their "Get Out Of School" album; just a bunch of cute kids whose music is harmless. I wonder how many parents would encourage their kids to promote this kind of message?

The danger of these ideas is probably best captured by Dr. Robert Demski, president of the Texas Society of Child and Adolescent Psychiatry. "Kids who hear songs over and over are desensitized to violence, sex, prostitution and drugs."

The debate about negative consequences on children, whether heard or seen, is over—even for kids who come from happy homes.

When a son or daughter argues that such lyrics or visuals will not change his or her behavior, remind them that support for such activity (purchasing CDs, movie tickets, or attending rock concerts) helps underwrite the production of this so-called entertainment. And, though such material may not directly change your children, the community and its residents will certainly suffer the consequences associated with immoral entertainment.

The challenge is to curtail "shock theatre" before children shock their parents.

Danika

June 4

Dear Mir, Montana Parent's Group:

I thought it was time to review recent issues discussed with Danika and Darcee.

ON ENTERTAINMENT: Though the purpose may be the same, the content is assuredly different than what we experienced as children. Are our children more worldly because of what they see on the screen, hear on the school bus, or read in the library? Or, is it possible that such sophistication is just an evolutionary phase passed on from generation to generation? In either case, does this legitimize the entertainment and news industries' decision to shock, desensitize, or embarrass? Is it necessary to tell all? Show all? Doesn't society (including children) run the risk of repeating Rome's appetite for destruction? If the public is really thirsting for such debauchery, why do G and PG-rated movies draw more people and profit? Why is there constant demand for responsible programming, free of unnecessary violence, language, and sexual escapades? Why does survey after survey demand a return to the family values and moral programming of yesteryear? And, ironically, why are there so many magazine articles, news reports, television talk shows and talk radio discussions about the decline of entertainment industry morals?

ON ROLE MODELS: Why are there relatively few heroes parents can recommend to their children? Police officers are held up to intense scrutiny by the press when their self-defense story may in fact be motivated by racial intolerance. Teachers go on strike. Doctors charge too much. Lawyers are dishonest. Televangelists are frauds . . . and on and on. Are there no heroes anymore? Even the Pope, with all his goodness, is a topic for reporters who probe to find out what His Holiness thinks of fallen-away Catholics or pedophilic priests. Can't the media identify positive role models who are not holding press conferences to announce that they're HIV positive? If the news and entertainment elite cannot decide what a role model should be, then parents must play a more proactive role. If mom and dad can't trust everyday strangers, why would they trust powerful idols whose products often tempt the prurient and materialistic interests of the young?

ON FREEDOM OF SPEECH: What parent would not give up freedom of speech opportunities in return for protecting their child from inappropriate language? Would a father seriously object to not having his son or daughter exposed to pornographic art, movies, or talk shows about the sexual habits of homosexuals? Does it make sense to tolerate public hate or nudity because of a misunderstood amendment? Surely the authors of our Constitution did not foresee the extremes their intentions have fostered. Is there no limit to tolerance? Must a nation exempt freedom of speech and freedom of expression from common sense?

ON DRAWING THE LINE: Related to freedoms, one must inquire why graphically violent and sexually explicit material continue to test the revised limits of decency. Why do the networks show more and more skin at earlier and earlier times? Why are TV talk show producers continually coming up with one bizarre quest after another? Is there anything indecent which hasn't been put to music, submitted as art, or discussed by shock jocks? Are ratings that important? Does childhood not matter? Are we not fueling the production of future Ted Bundys?

ON MEDIA BIAS: Why is it that the news industry has such a hard time finding positive stories to write? Cannot a single priest be found who is not a pedophile? Are there any celebrities whose contribution to charity represents a real sacrifice, not a token of their multi-millionaire salary? Are there no children who would be happy to espouse the merits of a G-rated Disney film? Can a sports star be found who is proud to be a role model to kids while communicating the merits of abstinence? Must every news team rush to the courtroom to cover juicy details about the sexual adventures of Hollywood personalities? Could we not rid our TV screens of abortion demonstrators and instead focus on the beauty of life? Could the news industry report on what's good in the world, free of political ideology and other hidden agendas? In short, could we have a bias for good?

My dear parents, I sincerely hope my questions will strengthen your resolve to continue your parenting journey. Hopefully, you will avoid Hell's heroes along the way.

Paul, Town Elder

Chapter Four

To Face the Wind

❀ ————————————————————————

Of all the gifts I could have given my children, I am proud of but one. I have prepared them to face the wind.
—Jay Willett, Phoenix, AZ
Back To The Family Parent

Part I
Dungeons, Dragons, and Diversity

Virtue is its own reward.
—Cicero

————————————————————————

19 June

Dear Darcee and Danika:

Though I may have a few years before I need worry about the sexual habits of my children, I can't help but be concerned. Cultural diversity, feminism and other movements will surely impact my kids. How can we protect our children from immorality?

Gillie

————————————————————————

22 June

Dear Gillie:

Maybe parents should do less worrying and more listening. In a report on teen pregnancy issued by the House

Select Committee on Children, Youth, and Families, researchers found that there has been a huge increase in the
number of teens who are sexually active.

It's going to happen. It has always happened. Only
now, kids are more sophisticated. They better understand
the physical maturity of their bodies. As parents, our job
is not to waste time preaching abstinence when the prob-
ability of that message being adopted is slim. It's one
thing to support virginity, it's quite another to be held
accountable for pregnancy, abortion, death.

Reality demands logical solutions. School-based clinics
offering condoms and counseling effectively help kids discover their sexuality. Teaching kids that sex is beautiful is
a welcome change from a society which still clings to the
absurdity of "victorian virtues."

Some children will save themselves for marriage, but
they are the kids who are generally unpopular in school.
And, if they do find a partner, they won't be prepared to
satisfy their mate. This is one reason why so many marriages fail.

Sexual enrichment begins with education. Why not
counsel young children on the gift of human sexuality?
One organization, Sex Information & Education Council
of the US (SIECUS) is now offering the kind of curriculum
our nation's schools should teach. Kids as young as five
can experience the wonderful gift of their bodies. By the
time these students reach puberty they are well prepared
to experience what they've learned. Following are examples
of the SIECUS message for children ages five to eight.

• Both girls and boys have body parts that feel good
when touched.

• Sexual intercourse occurs when a man and a woman
place the penis inside the vagina.

• Some men and women are homosexual, which means
they will be attracted to, and fall in love with, someone of
the same gender.

• Many gay men and lesbian women live in lifetime
committed relationships, even though they may not be
recognized as married.

- Children need help from adults to make some decisions.
- Everyone, including children, has rights.
- Masturbation should be done in a private place.
- Adults often kiss, hug, touch, and engage in other sexual behavior with one another to show caring and to share sexual pleasure.
- Intercourse is a pleasurable activity for most adults.
- A woman faced with an unintended pregnancy can carry the pregnancy to term and raise the baby, or place the baby for adoption, or have an abortion to end the pregnancy.

SIECUS will help inform children that sex is pleasurable and that tolerance and understanding are virtues worth practicing. Parents should do the same.

Darcee

---

22 June

Dear Gillie:

Parents can choose condoms or they can choose common sense. School-based clinics offering teen health information would seem a reasonable choice. Yet, across the country the presence of such facilities has a direct correlation with ballooning pregnancy, abortion, and sexually transmitted disease rates.

Passing out condoms to school children is the solution for those who continue to push sexual liberation. Unfortunately, many kids will not use a condom. Furthermore, many condoms fail, with sometimes fatal consequences for partners and/or their offspring.

Sex education curricula, like school-based clinics, seemingly provide safe answers to parents troubled by the potential promiscuous behavior of their kids.

Parents are told the answer lies in youth education. Sex experts teach the kids while Hollywood, music, and sports celebrities reinforce immoral behavior.

What proponents of hedonism fail to mention is that condoms and sex education classes refuse to consider the morality of such choices. Most schools won't teach values. Yet, experts will argue that kids are looking for answers. Then, when abstinence is suggested, these same intellectuals cry foul as the "A" word is accused of representing a hidden agenda for right-wing fanatics. Meanwhile, more than twenty-six thousand teens attend a pro-abstinence convention in Kentucky, fifty thousand people write Focus On The Family declaring their position against safe sex, and three out of four girls fifteen and under are still virgins.

Why? Could it be many young people believe sex is a gift from God, not to be abused? Is it possible there are teenagers who reject the condom argument as nothing more than promiscuity with consequences? If parents don't speak out against Sodom and Gomorrah television, directors like Steven Bocho ("NYPD Blue") will continue to push decency further into the background. Incest will be understood. Pedophilia will become a "right" if both parties agree (adult and child). Rape will be seen as a courtship stage. Homosexual sex will be viewed before, during, and after prime-time hours. Gangs like the "Spur Posse" will be commonplace, with sexual conquests perceived as nothing more than normal adolescent behavior.

What can parents do? First, recognize that virtue is right, while its adversary, promiscuity, is wrong. Second, become educated on the abstinence arguments. Read Focus On The Family's In Defense of A Little Virginity advertisement, which appeared in hundreds of newspapers across the country.

This message measured the return on investment in "safe sex." The results will open the eyes of even the most staunch condom supporters. In addition to presenting documentation on sexually transmitted diseases, Focus on the Family challenges the reader to weigh the moral consequences facing teens and parents.

Parents should also order a brochure from the City of New York which touts a "Teenager's Bill of Rights." Six tenets represent the reason why today's sexually active teenager is both confused and in trouble. Pray for the teenager who blindly accepts:

- I have the right to think for myself.
- I have the right to decide whether to have sex and whom to have it with.
- I have the right to use protection when I have sex.
- I have the right to buy and use condoms.
- I have the right to express myself.
- I have the right to ask for help if I need it.

It's time to lead our kids out of the immoral dungeon before the dragon devours them.

Danika

25 June

Dear Darcee and Danika:

Clearly, parents must be prepared to stand up for what they believe is right, regardless of so-called children's rights. Darcee, I would suggest that you carefully read Danika's letter and, in particular, a "Teenagers Bill of Rights." You will understand why many parents think common sense must prevail at the expense of senseless condoms.

An issue related to teenage sex is homosexuality. Many parents cringe when gay and lesbian issues surface in the news or on TV sitcoms. Yet, more and more children seem somewhat indifferent to the issue. Increasingly, parents have shared that their kids express little concern over the homosexual agenda—even to the point of defending gay men and lesbian women's rights to public displays of affection.

Such attitudes worry me. Will my children eventually accept what I believe is morally wrong? Am I right to be concerned? What position should God-fearing parents take on cultural diversity?

Gillie

---

25 June

Dear Gillie:

I took your advice and read Danika's commentary on the "Teenagers Bill of Rights." I then read your 25 June correspondence. I wonder, who's really confused? But let's ignore this issue for now, and deal with your homophobia.

Gillie, you asked, "What position should God-fearing parents take on cultural diversity?" Realize that intolerance of gay rights represents a serious threat to children of bigoted parents. May I suggest you recall God's warning, "Judge not, lest ye be judged."

There are several reasons why young people unconditionally accept homosexuality. Because of media coverage, there is a greater respect for, and understanding of, gay men and lesbian women. Respect is demonstrated by countless military heroes who have had to hide their sexual preference from company commanders. Respect is captured on the face of lesbian moms who are experiencing successful parenthood. Respect is earned by thousands of gay youths who struggle to be accepted by peers and loved by parents.

Times have changed, Gillie. In your day young people opened the eyes of racist parents who had to learn that "all men were created equal." Today, a similar fight is being won by progressive teens who recognize that homophobia is a sin!

Ask parents of homosexual teens how they feel about their children. Talk with the dad whose homosexual son died for his country. Listen to clergy who weep for fellow brothers and sisters whose religion forbids gay men and lesbian women from preaching the word of God.

Homophobia at any level is wrong. That's why courts are beginning to recognize the civil rights of homosexuals.

Groups like the Boy Scouts are questioned on prejudicial policies forbidding gay Scout Leaders. It doesn't matter that the leader may be an Eagle Scout, having earned multiple merit badges. Organizations like Levi Strauss and Wells Fargo see this policy for what it is, and, as a result, the Boy Scouts have lost thousands of dollars in sponsorship monies.

Fortunately, progress is being made. Diversity training is available on college campuses and in corporate board rooms. Legal challenges are mounting in an effort to punish those who would discriminate against homosexual marriages. Scientists are reporting definitive evidence that one's genetic makeup may well account for sexual preference. And Hollywood script writers and news reporters continue the education process with real life stories about the consequences homophobia brings to an intolerant America. Thanks to organizations like SIECUS, our children will learn that homosexual love is love! And, if a youth is confused about his or her sexual orientation, there will be plenty of professionals who will provide direction in the child's search for truth.

I pray that parents will recognize that homosexuality is not a moral issue, but homophobia is.

Darcee

---

28 June

Dear Gillie:

"Cultural diversity" has such a non-threatening, almost pleasant sound. It literally means having the ability to recognize and respect differences across sexes, races, and ethnic groups. Proponents suggest that discrimination against Jews, blacks, or homosexuals is equally wrong. They mention gay rights and civil rights in the same breath. These defenders of diversity demand tolerance of homosexual acts and lifestyles.

But, should sexual preference deserve the same protection as civil or human rights? Does the color of one's

skin tell us anything about his character? Does the fact
that a person is Jewish provide clues as to how he or she
will act behind closed doors? When a person openly practices homosexuality, doesn't such behavior give us a picture as to the moral strength of that individual? And, if
sexual preferences must be protected, then why all the
fuss about pedophilia? All pedophiles want is the "right"
to have sex with young boys. Why stop there? Bestiality or
necrophilia, anyone?

Gillie, parents everywhere should be concerned that
the homosexual lobby wants congress to allow two gay
men or lesbian women the right to raise children. They
want sodomy laws eliminated from the books. They demand that military leaders look the other way. And, they
insist that educational institutions indoctrinate children to
believe that homosexuality is an alternative way to love a
human being. This agenda is a conscious conspiracy to
move away from heterosexual love as the only moral choice
available.

If gay rights are universally accepted by authorities,
parents are in for a rough ride. Prepare for increased
media attention covering lifestyles of the gay and lesbian
community; network psychologists offering commentary
on the homophobia disease and how to cure it; prime-
time movies featuring bedroom scenes with gay men inches
away from sodomy; prosecutors asking the jury for harsh
sentences for individuals who had an altercation with a
homosexual, basing their case on the "hate crime" argument; family adoption agencies scrambling to find lesbian
couples their first child; public displays of affection between homosexual lovers; citizens paying higher taxes for
an even higher AIDS epidemic; Boy Scout troops forced
to compromise their principles by allowing gay men the
"right" to sleep with young scouts; campus diversity policies forbidding students the right to request a heterosexual roommate; and children taught that homosexuality
is normal; courtesy of your state supported gay and lesbian center.

Senator Moynihan of New York correctly defines such deviant behavior as "moral deregulation." How far will the tolerance industry go? Currently, AIDS carriers are protected by privacy laws. As a result, patients of HIV-positive doctors will never know the risk. Police officers bitten by an intravenous drug user may not inquire as to the risk of contracting AIDS. Meanwhile, young people brainwashed by diversity dogma increase their tolerance for homosexual practices including sodomy, orgies, sadomasochism, and pedophilia.

In the SIECUS booklet, "Guidelines for Comprehensive Sexuality Education," adolescents are reminded: "Parents, teachers, guidance counselors, physicians, religious leaders, and gay and lesbian community centers may offer support for young people who have concerns about their sexual orientation."

Perhaps we should ask Darcee why the above statement lists only the gay and lesbian switchboard number.

Gillie, before your children can be expected to defend what you believe is morally right, they must first be taught what is morally wrong. And the best way to achieve the latter is to read Paul's letters to the Romans (Rom. 1:26-27), Timothy (1 Tim. 1:9-10), and Corinthians (1 Cor. 6:9). If parents take the initiative, future generations may reverse Solzyhenitsyn's observation: "Men have forgotten God, that's why all these things happened."

Danika

Part II
Of Censorship and Sponsorship

Every society has a right to preserve public peace and order, and therefore has a good right to prohibit the propagation of opinions which have a dangerous tendency.
—Samuel Johnson
18th Century Writer

1 July

Dear Darcee and Danika:

Every time Brina and I talk to our teenager about the dangers of pornography or drugs, she reminds us that censorship is the greater evil. To our way of thinking it would be better to censor pornographic materials, drugs, and hate groups from our children, than to worry about losing an immoral freedom.

How should parents justify censorship to their kids? Is there a way to get the point across without actually demanding the removal of inappropriate messages or images? Many parents eagerly await your response.

Brina and Hasheem

5 July

Dear Brina and Hasheem:

Perhaps you remember a man by the name of Adolf Hitler. This man knew if he could control what is taught in schools, censoring all beliefs contrary to his own, he could rule the people. He said, "Let me control the textbooks and I will control Germany."

Scary, huh? Imagine for a moment that your local library was picketed by right wingers who felt that your children should not read certain books or watch certain videos. How would you feel? What would you do? Fundamentalists would be telling you how to raise your children. Such episodes are happening across the country.

Next thing you know, adults will not be permitted access to material with adult themes. Even now, individuals with an interest in nude portraits of young children have been branded as child pornographers. And, though some authorities will argue that child pornography is against the law, organizations like the American Civil Liberties Union are correct when they take the position that once such material is in the marketplace, citizens should have the legal right to purchase whatever they deem appropriate. Failure to do so is censorship. John Cummings, spokesman for the ACLU's Art Censorship Project says, "There is no evidence that seeing or reading this material leads to child molestation." And isn't that the point? Why censor the rights of one group or individual because some parents are afraid of what has yet to be proven?

I can't help but wonder how many of these same "worry warts" have teenagers who participated in a recent survey where more than 84 percent of girls admitted to watching pornography. Should their parents condemn them for having a healthy interest in sex? I think not.

Censorship is everywhere. From movie ratings to warning labels, someone is telling you what they think your kid should read, see or hear. Never mind that your values may be different; forget that you've taught the kids right from wrong; ignore the fact that your family's rights are violated.

Censor art and you destroy the National Endowment for the Arts. Censor a library book and you close your public library. Censor a rock group and the music will die. If not checked, you and your children will discover that demands for a puritanical society will lead to the destruction of our nation's freedoms.

Your daughter is right—censorship is the greater evil. Censor her freedom and you run the risk of violating your daughter.

Darcee

---

5 July

Dear Brina and Hasheem:

You've heard it before. Screaming "fire" in a crowded theatre is not permitted. Is this not censorship? Of course it is. Every time a parent chooses not to allow his or her child to see something, hear something, attend something, buy something, or read something, that parent is practicing censorship.

In fact, every time parents say no, their child is experiencing some form of censorship. Thank God!

Morality In Media, Inc. has created a series of cliches used to expose myths surrounding the censorship argument.

MYTH: Freedom of expression is protected by the First Amendment.

REALITY: The United States Supreme Court consistently has held that obscenity is not protected by the First Amendment, any more than libel, perjury, slander, contempt of court, false advertising, or copyright violations are.

MYTH: You cannot legislate morality.

REALITY: On face value, this cliche is absurd and an argument against the democratic process itself. All law rests on moral assumption, and every law legislates morality.

MYTH: Are you imposing morality on me?

REALITY: In any society, someone's morality (or immorality) must prevail. The real question becomes, "Whose morality will prevail in America?" The pornographers, leading to anarchy and decadence, or the moral principles of those who honor the Judeo-Christian code—a code which has been embraced, not imposed, as the cornerstone of Western civilization?

MYTH: What next? Where do you draw the line? A ban on obscene materials today will lead to the real censorship tomorrow with maybe the Bible being banned next.

REALITY: Such absurdities are somewhat like being asked to believe that a ban against playing loud rock music at 3 A.M., in the midst of a residential street, would lead to a ban on the right of the Philharmonic to perform at Carnegie Hall.

MYTH: Pornography is thriving, so the American people must want it or accept it.

REALITY: All surveys show that the majority of Americans are vehemently opposed to traffic in pornography and want it stopped.

MYTH: Pornography is a victimless crime.

REALITY: Children are victimized in a myriad of ways. Some are used in child pornographic materials to "soften them up" for incest and other sexual molestation.

MYTH: Why be concerned about obscenity when there is so much violent crime?

REALITY: They're related. It is not coincidence that when adult bookstores are closed down, violent crimes decrease in that neighborhood due to an exodus of prostitutes, drug pushers, and the criminally prone who are attracted to pornography outlets.

MYTH: It is up to parents to supervise their children and protect them from exposure to indecent broadcasting.

REALITY: There is no feasible way for parents to protect their children from exposure to indecent programming short of confining a child or teenager twenty-four hours a day in a soundproof isolation unit without radio or TV.

MYTH: If you don't want to be exposed to indecent programs on radio or TV, turn the dial.

REALITY: The U.S. Supreme Court has rejected the "turn-the-dial" argument. Because the broadcast audience is constantly tuning in and out, prior warnings cannot completely protect the listener or viewer from unexpected program content.

If the reality responses are perceived as too technical, then educate your teenage daughter about "Chester the Molester." Chester was the brainchild of cartoonist Dwaine Tinsley who produced 145 child abuse cartoons for *Hustler* magazine. In an interview for a video called "Rate It X," Mr. Tinsley described Chester the Molester as "this dirty old guy who would do anything to trap a young girl . . . the younger ones, 10 or 12. He would lay out candy for them like he was trying to trap . . . a bird." Mr. Tinsley was eventually arrested for child sexual abuse.

Remind your daughter that The National Coalition For The Protection Of Children & Families has an affiliated organization known as "Enough Is Enough!" According to this group there are more hard-core porn outlets than McDonalds, 8,800 to 15,000; the smut industry grosses 8 to 10 billion annually; a woman is raped every forty-six seconds; and the serial child molester will abuse up to 380 children in his lifetime.

If this doesn't do it, pick up a copy of the video "Bleed Little Girl Bleed" and watch it with your daughter. When she sees a six-year-old girl being raped, the censorship argument will self-destruct. Hopefully, your teenager and others like her will come to understand that censoring pornography is not the issue. Sponsoring pornography is.

Danika

---

8 July

Dear Darcee and Danika:

Censoring both hard and soft-core pornography makes sense to us. Clearly, violence against women and children is due, in part, to the spreading of such filth.

Danika, you mentioned that sponsorship, not censorship, is the central issue. Several parents in our group were curious if the same rationale applies to racist organizations like the Ku Klux Klan. If parents fail to demand the censoring of hate groups, are moms and dads in effect condoning these organizations?

Darcee, we would like to know how you feel about Danika's "sponsorship" position.

And, to both of you, please comment on the drug legalization issue.

Brina and Hasheem

---

11 July

Dear Brina and Hasheem:

I emphatically state censorship in any form is wrong. This position does not mean that violence against women and children is right. But, I firmly believe that once you cross the line and make exceptions, the door is open for the total loss of freedom.

Having said this, I would like to tackle the drug legalization issue. Drugs in the wrong hands can destroy communities. Young children should never be exposed to drugs of any kind. But, for adolescents and teenagers, we must carefully analyze the situation.

Smoking is a common occurrence among youth. Experts argue that this habit is addictive. But, unlike marijuana, cocaine, or heroin, tobacco is not a controlled substance. Cigarette smoking is legal.

Alcohol is another example. If not controlled, certain young people could become alcoholics. Yet, many cultures condone a glass of wine or two at the dinner table for all family members. In America, it is very common for parents to give their teenagers a beer at home. Progressive adults recognize that little harm can come from this privilege.

Though heroin and cocaine are very dangerous, marijuana is nothing more than a mind relaxant with little or no consequences. Yet, the cost of chasing weed pushers is staggering.

In 1993 over ninety thousand youth were arrested for drug law violations. Many of these "criminals" were teenagers smoking marijuana for enjoyment. This drug is not addictive. You can't get cancer. You can drive, take exams, and do your job. So what's the problem?

Why spend millions of dollars chasing kids who smoke a joint? Why not invest this money in education or in finding a cure for AIDS? The war on drugs has failed. For every marijuana plant burned, ten more sprout up. For every dealer convicted, five more take his place. Even parents, who condemn their children for recreational drug use, enjoy the same pleasure.

If you allow kids to smoke or enjoy a glass of wine at dinner, why overreact to a harmless hallucinogenic?

Now to the sponsorship theory. This argument is a

fancy term for skirting around the censorship issue. Let's call a spade a spade. If you object to a radical group's First Amendment privilege, then you are practicing censorship. What if, instead of the KKK, the censor patrol opted to silence the Catholic Church? Would you speak up in Rome's defense? Would you demand authorities uphold the Constitution? Would you become a martyr for the faith?

Because others have a different set of beliefs, doesn't mean you shouldn't be tolerant. Every time an Aryan Nation representative speaks at a rally for youth, parents panic. Yet, much of this group's message focuses on God and country. The problem many parents have is the innate fear that some cult will recruit their children away. Only incompetent parents need worry. And even then, their kids may be better off.

If you don't believe the censorship issue has gotten out of hand, consider this: The American Library Association has actively cautioned its members to be on guard against those who would censor your children's right to read or view certain materials.

When censorship (sponsorship) gets to the point of policing the local library or judging other's right to free expression of ideas, we have gone too far.

Ultimately, your teenage daughter and her generation will never stand for this.

Darcee

---

11 July

Dear Brina and Hasheem:

Sponsorship is often fueled by complacency. The latter term literally means "a feeling of contentment with an unawareness of danger or trouble." Parents who allow sons and daughters to buy rock music with sexually explicit or violent lyrics, often justify their decision on the position that their child would never imitate such behaviors. Unfortunately, what parents have done is sponsor the proliferation of immoral music. Though their child may not seduce and rape another, some kid, somewhere, will. By not acting, parents have, in effect, endorsed the consequences.

The same can be said for a society which allows groups like the KKK to spew their racist remarks in public. By hiding behind the freedom-of-speech argument, anti-censorship groups end up endorsing hate. Consider the irony in the term censor. According to the *American Heritage Dictionary*, a censor is: "a person authorized to examine books, films or other material and to remove or suppress what is considered morally, politically or otherwise objectionable." Given the definition, doesn't it seem odd that the American Library Association has a department with the title, Office of Intellectual Freedom. According to Cal Thomas, in his article, "Censors Scream Loudest About Censorship," one of the department's dictates states: "no one may make a moral judgment for anyone else." Now, if the library doesn't censor materials, then how does the institution decide what books and videos to buy? Aren't they choosing to sponsor some piece of literature or film, while rejecting others?

Every day some form of censorship is exploited in the classroom, courtroom, or home. Anytime a parent prohibits a child from doing something, that parent has become a censor.

To your other question about drug legalization, may I suggest the argument that, free access will diminish crime, conveniently ignores the consequences of a "drugged" society. Drug legalization presupposes that limits will be put on what can be purchased, in what quantity, and by whom. History will show that once the moral standard is lowered, no perversion is objectionable. All one has to do is follow the TV industry's record for permitting violence and sexual promiscuity on the screen. Such permissiveness guarantees no limits and no measure of what is right or wrong.

If standing up for what you believe labels parents as censors, so be it. Better to censor what is wrong, than to sponsor what is evil.

Danika

Part III
Blacks and Whites and Shades of Gray

Suffer the little children to come unto me, and forbid them not; for of such is the Kingdom of God.

—Mark 10:14

---

14 July

Dear Darcee and Danika:

When we gaze at our grandchildren we can't help but wonder how our lives would be without them. When I was pregnant there was never any discussion about abortion. We never questioned whether we could afford to raise the child. We were prepared to give up our freedom. I was ready for my "motherhood" career.

Today too many young people seem to be indifferent to the meaning of life. What should parents teach their children about abortion? And more important, what should be taught about the sanctity of life?

Jan and Richard

---

17 July

Dear Jan and Richard:

Let's begin this conversation with reality. Did you know that U.S. Catholic Bishops emphasize that "abortion" is but one of 14 issues the voting public should weigh when selecting a candidate for office? What does this say when the leading anti-choice institution in the country fails to lead the charge? Maybe that's why poll after poll supports the pro-choice initiative. Perhaps it has something to do with a citizens' right to privacy.

Over the last 20 years we have heard one silly anti-choice argument after the other: "It's immoral." "Life begins at conception." "A woman has no right to control her body."

It matters little if the lady has been raped; the birth of the fetus may kill her; the family can't afford another mouth to feed; the girl who's pregnant is not yet ready to handle the responsibility; the child would be handicapped; or there's no father, or worse yet, he's a drug addict. None of this matters to self-righteous pulpit preachers who would be the first to rush their raped daughter to the hospital for an abortion.

A woman must raise a child with or without the father. But to religious fanatics, it's irrelevant that medical bills will bankrupt the family. Such hypocrisy among the clergy and other radical factions represent a serious danger to society.

Here's a litmus test for religious fanatics who charge that pro-choice advocates are murderers. Ask your local Catholic abortion clinic picketer if she would rather raise a homosexual child who would die of AIDS and eventually end up in Hell; or, abort the child to live in eternal paradise. Watch the confusion.

Challenge any father who states he would never encourage his unmarried daughter to abort his future retarded grandchild. Ask this same man if he would prefer to see his "little girl" live in poverty. The issue is not "sanctity of life." The issue is how to protect a woman's God-given right to choose what is best for her body, her family, her lifestyle, her psyche.

Point out to your children that as they grow "choices" will be forthcoming. Among them may be the decision to abort a fetus. Do not paint this choice as evil. Abortion is just another family alternative.

And finally, remind your kids that "choice" begins with life.

Darcee

17 July

Dear Jan and Richard:

This country is rapidly approaching 37 million abortions since the passage of *Roe versus Wade*. Abortion, thought to be the alternative to back-alley surgeries, has quickly become a "matter of convenience." With media personalities reporting positive abortion stories, and TV movies glorifying a woman's right to choose, is it any wonder that so many young people are confused?

Too many pregnant teens see abortion as a way to avoid their parents or keep the boyfriend. They see abortion as their "right" irrespective of the father's feelings and that the child is a gift from God.

If the pro-choice physician senses an interest in abortion, the conversation quickly centers around the "fetus." If the same doctor perceives the patient wishes to have the child, the fetus is given the title "baby." The question isn't, "Have you felt your fetus kick?"

Too many judges are prepared to force states to honor the privacy of a teen over the parental jurisdiction of her parents. Ironically, she may not receive an aspirin from health professionals without parental approval even though medical personnel may abort her child without her mother or father's knowledge.

Such logic is even more bizarre when you consider that several judges, special interest groups, and legislators refuse to support a 24-hour "think it over" period. These "scholars" have even agreed to lift any restriction forbidding abortions where the child ("fetus") has a chance to survive. Technically your daughter may abort your future grandchild right up to delivery!

Sadly, abortionists ignore the medical community's Hippocratic Oath of 400 B.C. The oath states: "I will give no deadly medicine to anyone if asked, nor suggest any such counsel. Furthermore, I will not give a woman an instrument to produce abortion."

You asked what parents should teach their children about abortion. Begin with "sanctity of life." Tell your children that all human life is precious. Explain that life begins at conception and ends at death. Remind them that parents have a responsibility to care for and love all children regardless of . . . the health of the baby . . . the financial condition of the family . . . the circumstances of conception . . . or any other rationale one might use to justify abortion.

And finally, share the following with your sons and daughters.

> When God wants an important thing done in this world or a wrong righted, He goes about it in a very singular way. He doesn't release thunderbolts, or stir up earthquakes. God simply has a tiny baby born, perhaps of a very humble home, perhaps of a very humble mother. And God puts the idea or purpose into the mother's heart. And she puts it in the baby's mind, and then—God waits. The great events of this world are not battles and elections and earthquakes or thunderbolts. The great events are babies, for each child comes with the message that God is not yet discouraged with humanity, but is still expecting goodwill to become incarnate in each human life. (Anonymous)

Danika

---

20 July

Dear Darcee and Danika:

There are related concerns surrounding "sanctity of life" issues. Three hot buttons are euthanasia, cloning and using aborted fetal tissue for transplants.

Has medical science crossed the line? Will our children or grandchildren eventually play God, deciding who lives, who dies, what's a perfect child, and what to do with the discarded parts?

Jan and Richard

23 July

Dear Jan and Richard:

Imagine if medical science had not elected to develop artificial insemination, or in-vitro fertilization. How many couples would still be childless? Suppose progressive surgeons backed off using lumpectomies, choosing instead radical mastectomies. How many unhappy women would there be? Or how about mammography? There was a time when many in the medical community felt that radiation exposure posed too much risk. Imagine how many smokers would have died if the medical profession had listened to Dr. Max Cutler, an American cancer surgeon who in 1954 stated, "I feel strongly that the blanket statements which appeared in the press that there is a direct and causative relation between smoking of cigarettes, and the number of cigarettes smoked, to cancer of the lung is an absolutely unwarranted conclusion." Could the science of cloning represent the future eradication of genetically inherited diseases? If aborted fetal tissue is used for bone marrow transplants or skin grafts, can one suggest that this is evil? And as seniors begin to deteriorate physically, is there not a need for "death with dignity" options?

Let's look at each issue separately. What parents wouldn't want a "beautiful" child? How about one with an IQ of 150? Would moms and dads refuse offspring who were artistically or athletically gifted? And what about health? Wouldn't mothers and fathers prefer a child with little chance of genetic disorders?

This is what cloning is all about. The science of genetic mapping potentially will produce a race of children with desirable traits. Imagine boys with the athletic ability of Michael Jordan; or girls with the physical attractiveness of Cindy Crawford. If cloning helps couples conceive a perfect child, then surely such advancements are blessed by God. Though some will argue that cloning is playing God, I will argue that cloning is God's gift to the human race.

The same is true for the medical professional who dares to transplant one or more fetal parts to the body of a living child. Does this not parallel the miracles of Jesus who brought sight to the blind or hearing to the deaf? Who among us would prefer to live in constant pain, often at the expense of bankrupting our family? Is there not a time when euthanasia is appropriate? What's the difference between pregnancy termination for a Down's syndrome fetus and ending a life in agony? Don't both examples represent mercy? If there wasn't a demand for euthanasia, why are celebrities like Dr. Kevorkian continually in the news? Why did the book *Final Exit* make the best-seller list? Why does the Hemlock Society continue to add new members? Jan, would you want to see Richard suffer? Richard, would you deny Jan her right to free her family from unforgiving medical bills? A compassionate God would forgive either of you for loving the other enough to end their misery. This same God understands the need for fetal transplants, cloning and abortion.

In each case the issue is not "right to life," but, "right to choose." Were it not so, God would not have introduced the technology designed to free our world from unwanted pregnancies, diseased and handicapped children, or senior citizens who are a burden to society.

Darcee

---

23 July

Dear Jan and Richard:

Remember when abortion became legal? The year was 1973. The argument centered around a woman's right to do with her body as she pleased. Elimination of back-alley surgical death was the goal. Ironic isn't it? To save a few, millions have died.

Ten years after the Supreme Court decision, another genocide license was granted when a Bloomington, Indiana court ruled that parents may starve to death a Down's syndrome child. His name was Baby Doe. Across the state line, a Michigan doctor made national headlines because he helped people die. Compassion was the reason, he said.

As society continues to tolerate right-to-die initiatives, more and more of the helpless of our nation become victims. Children in the womb with less than a perfect mind or body are candidates for sacrifice. Children whose mother forgot to take the pill . . . whose father is unemployed . . . whose parents want freedom . . . whose sex is wrong . . . are all at risk. Of course there's always cloning—the embryo supermarket of the future. Photo and ID reports would be displayed in a mail order catalogue. "Designer clones" would fetch a premium.

Fetal body parts represent another product line. Teenage girls choosing an abortion can make money if they wait long enough, ensuring full development of the baby's organs. With transplant doctors standing by, and organ dealers and their buyers ready to negotiate, business will blossom. Fetal part-finder fees will be common, giving new meaning to "body part shops."

Bizarre? Don't kid yourself. When you were both young, a madman by the name of Adolf Hitler masterminded a plot to eliminate those who didn't measure up to "superior race" specifications. Undesirables included Jews, Gypsies, the old, retarded, deformed, and non-Aryan wealthy living in the Fatherland.

The German people denied allied accusations of mass extermination until the horrors of Auschwitz were revealed. Their sin was tolerance. And if this nation is not careful, we may well fulfill political philosopher William Burke's prediction. "This country is plunging headlong into a science-fiction nightmare; in the final analysis, fetal tissue implants are not that much different from Nazi lampshades made of Jewish skin. Both intend to put by-products of murder to good use."

While all this is going on, there is no guarantee grandparents will be around. Euthanasia is to the old what abortion is to the young. If society's sense of morality justifies the destruction of the unborn, why should it tolerate unproductive citizens whose health care bills add to the national debt?

These nightmarish scenarios are not unique to the womb and tomb generations. If abortion clinics represent "solution centers" for teenage girls, what's to stop the creation of suicide centers for the unhappy teen? If sanctioned by the courts as a right-to-choose alternative, parents or grandparents will, at best, learn of the tragedy after the fact!

Technology is not the concern. Morality is. As General Omar Bradley said, "We have grasped the mystery of the atom and rejected the Sermon on the Mount."

Danika

Part IV
In Search of Symbiosis

One of the most touching stories about the American Revolution was that of a British officer who somehow got separated from his unit and was trying to make his way back to camp silently through the trees. As he approached the trees he was startled to see an American general on his knees, hands clasped before his face in fervent prayer. As the Englishman looked on, his heart sank and tears came to his eyes for he saw the praying officer was General George Washington, commander of the American Forces. "When I saw the site," he said later, "I knew we were defeated. For any army whose commander was so humble before Almighty God could never lose the war."

---

26 July

Dear Darcee and Danika:

There seems to be a cultural war brewing around the First Amendment.

Interpretation of our nation's forefathers' intent has appeared to disrupt courts, schools, politicians and the media. Please help us understand the issues swirling around "separation of church and state."

John & Ronica

---

29 July

Dear John and Ronica:

Ever wonder why the pilgrims left England? It wasn't just taxes. Religion, the King's religion, had a lot to do with the escape to the new land.

The First Amendment phrase that has entangled society is "Congress shall make no law respecting an establishment of religion, or prohibiting the free exercise thereof." On the surface these few words appear to protect citizens from a state-sponsored religion.

But it's not that simple. The gentlemen who wrote the Constitution could not have foreseen the influence of the Catholic Church; envisioned how TV evangelism would rip off a naive public; imagined the earning power of Jewish elite; or understood how the minds of children can be manipulated through school-sponsored religious pageants, after-school Bible Study groups, or service club oaths forcing an allegiance to a supreme being.

Our nation's constitutional authors would have applauded Madeline O'Hara for demanding freedom from God. Washington, Jefferson, Adams, and others would be proud of the young lady who objected to a rabbi's prayer at her Junior High commencement. Her courage was vindicated when the highest court in the land agreed that invocations and benedictions at public schools are unconstitutional. And if our forefathers walked down Pennsylvania Avenue during the winter holiday break, they would notice that government offices were void of cluttering manger scenes, Menorahs or other religious paraphernalia.

Church and state must remain as far away from each other as possible. Religion has only one place—the church or synagogue where a free people can come and pray as they choose.

Religion does not belong before, during, or after school, or in any other environment outside traditional places of worship. I might also suggest that religion has a limited place in the home. If parents teach their children right from wrong, there is little need for forcing God down their throats.

If religious controls were absent, society would be forced to attend services, teach values in school, and pay taxes for statues honoring Billy Graham, Pope John Paul II, and Mother Theresa. Do you want that? Are you prepared for an inquisition of those who refuse to accept a state-sponsored god?

If this is truly the land of the free, then religion must not act as a barrier to our freedoms. When a denomination as powerful as the Roman Catholic Church can condemn women priests, homosexuals, the divorced, atheists, and religions out of the mainstream, freedom is in peril. When so-called men of God are arrested for sexual child abuse or misappropriation of funds, separation of church and state must stand.

Courts, lawmakers, and media have joined forces to protect your family from the potential dangers of religion. Your job is to protect your children from the same institution.

Darcee

---

29 July

Dear John and Ronica:

I would like to begin with some advice from both Alexis de Tocqueville, a French statesman, and war hero, General Douglas MacArthur. Tocqueville lived in the 1800's and was known for publishing *Democracy in America*, which he wrote after admiring the ideals of the new government. Though he praised the country for pursuing liberty and equality, he reminded his French colleagues, "Religion is more needed in democratic republics than in many others." He further stated, "Liberty in regard to religion is a safeguard of morality, and morality is the best security of law and the surest pledge of the duration of freedom."

MacArthur was more blunt. "History fails to record a single precedent in which nations subject to moral decay have not passed into political and economic decline. There has been either a spiritual awakening to overcome the moral lapse, or a progressive deterioration leading to ultimate national disaster."

The "establishment of religion" debate has reached absurdity. Those who would reinterpret the First Amendment's true meaning are pushing for a secular state, free of religious influence. Their dogma prohibits teaching Judeo-Christian principles.

On one hand Americans are reminded of the freedoms encouraged by great leaders of the past. On the other hand the public is told to ignore their forefathers' wisdom including "Praise Be To God" (Washington Monument); "Nation Under God" (Lincoln Memorial); "Liberty is a gift of God" (Jefferson Memorial). Following this logic, citizens should ignore the meaning behind "Endowed by the Creator," found in our Declaration of Independence; "One Nation Under God," recited in our Pledge of Allegiance; "God Shed His Grace on Thee," from "America the Beautiful"; and, "In God We Trust," found on all coins or legal tender.

Judeo-Christian morality represents a major influence in every facet of American culture. Our nation's traditions, laws, history, and values are a derivative of the principles set forth by the likes of Washington, Lincoln, Jefferson and Franklin.

Separation of church and state does not mean separation from God. When *Reader's Digest* ran a national poll, measuring the approval or disapproval of the U.S. Supreme Court's ruling that commencement prayer at High School graduation ceremonies is unconstitutional, fully 80 percent of the public disagreed. The findings demonstrated how out of touch the courts have become. Given that the Supreme Court begins each session with the words, "God save us and the Honorable Court," one would think the justices would take their own advice.

Instead, the highest court in the land has said "no" to commencement prayers, prayer in school and public manger scenes on government property. A national case illustrates the point. A Rhode Island teen upset an entire nation when she and her father took her case to the Supreme Court requesting that a Rabbi's prayer at commencement be forbidden as such activity violated the separation of church and state. In a 5:4 Supreme Court ruling, the majority said that the prayer constituted "psychological coercion" by forcing "subtle and indirect peer pressure" on unbelievers who, when asked to stand or maintain a respectful silence, face the dilemma of protesting or appearing to participate. This, the court claimed, qualifies as "establishment of religion."

George Will, syndicated columnist had this to say. "Is there not suddenly unconstitutional psychological coercion toward political orthodoxy in playing the National Anthem at sporting events? Is there not public and peer pressure to stand respectfully?" Will admonished, "see you in court."

In a survey of *Glamour* magazine readers, 82 percent replied that public displays of religion such as nativity scenes and Menorahs should be permitted; 75 percent said students should be allowed to attend Bible or prayer sessions on school property after school. Seventy-two percent said they wouldn't be offended by a public prayer at a graduation or football game.

The first question parents must ponder is whether the teaching of religious values strengthens our society; if not, separation of church and state is moot.

Perhaps the statement made by a Moscow councilman, "There are no values in our society," provides the answer. Maybe that's why Russia's state run schools now mandate teaching values.

In this country teachers can't discuss morality in the classroom for fear that the ACLU will sue. Teachers are expected to remain neutral while young people grapple for answers. These same youngsters may eventually turn to other educators like Hollywood. This scenario is especially frightening when a Media Research Center article entitled, "Hollywood: Losing Its Religion," reported that only 81 out of 1,462 speaking characters had an identifiable religious affiliation. Maybe that's why movies like *Going My Way* with Bing Crosby as Father O'Mally have been replaced with *The Pope Must Die*. Michael Medved, author of *Hollywood vs. America* and noted movie critic, refers to this phenomenon as "the separation of church and studio."

Parents who choose God—choose morality. Parents who choose to separate from God—choose chaos. Don't abdicate your rights. Demand that your children live in a moral society. The courts, schools, politicians and media have made their choice. It's time for parents to make theirs.

Danika

---

1 August

Dear Darcee and Danika:

Your positions on church and state are miles apart.

Darcee, we would encourage you to study Danika's letter with special emphasis on her final paragraph. Danika, thank you for sensitizing us to the seriousness of the First Amendment debate.

John & Ronica

4 August

Dear John and Ronica:

How does it feel to be brainwashed? I can't believe that bright parents would let Danika convince you that those who follow the law are in danger of violating God's commandments.

Didn't Jesus say, "Give to Ceasar what is Ceasar's, and to God what is God's?" Didn't he preach obedience? Were not the constitutional authors a religious people? Why then would you ignore their warning about the dangers of the church?

Look again at Danika's final paragraph. The first sentence suggests that only through God will you find morality. If this is true, why are there so many moral people in this country who have little or nothing to do with religion?

Must you marry in a church to prove you love your mate? Do you need religious training to know the difference between right and wrong? Is it imperative that a nativity scene be visible to sanction the winter holidays?

I found it interesting that Danika would ridicule the highest court in the land because she doesn't like the decisions handed down. What she failed to mention was that of all the blessings the American people have received, freedom (including freedom from religious oppression) is the greatest. Remember, Jesus told Pilate that authority comes from God. When Supreme Court justices uphold the law, they certainly are following the will of the Creator.

Another absurdity is Danika's criticism of the little girl from Rhode Island who dared to protect your freedom. Yes, I said your freedom. Her bravery against school authorities was astounding. The result—vindication.

Because of her courage, parents can be assured that their children will not be forced to pray to a god of someone else's choosing.

Girl Scouts are now permitted to substitute God in their oath for any deity they choose. Thus, a Moslem Girl

Scout will no longer be offended because Allah is ignored in favor of some Judeo-Christian image. Hopefully, an atheist Girl Scout will one day be allowed to promise: On my honor, I will try to serve my country, to help people at all times, and to live by the Girl Scout Law.

If you listen to Danika, she will have you voting against all this country stands for. Choose against the courts and you break the law. Choose private schools or home schooling and you destroy education. Choose against political winds and you face alienation.

If you want these outcomes for your children, choose Danika.

                                                        Darcee

---

                                            4 August

Dear John and Ronica:

Robert F. Drinan, in his book *The Fractured Dream: America's Divisive Moral Choices*, has an interesting way to describe the church and state controversy. He calls it symbiosis. As Drinan says, "That term means the living together, in an intimate way, of two dissimilar organisms in a mutually beneficial relationship."

It would seem that the following gentlemen were able to achieve such a relationship.

George Washington: "Of all the dispositions and habits which led to political prosperity, religion and morality are indispensable supports."

John Adams: "Our constitution was made only for a moral and religious people."

James Madison: "Before any man can be considered as a member of civil society, he must be considered as a subject of the governor of the universe."

Benjamin Franklin: "A good newspaper and Bible in every house, a good school house in every district, and a church in every neighborhood, all appreciated as they deserve, are the chief support of virtue, morality, civil liberty and religion."

Thomas Jefferson: "Can the liberties of a nation be thought secure when we have renounced their only firm basis, a conviction in the minds of the people that these liberties are the gift of God. Religion should be regarded as a supplement to the law and the government of man, and as the alpha and omega of the moral law."

This wisdom didn't begin in 1776. The pilgrims recorded on November 11, 1620, in the "Mayflower Compact":

> In the name of God, Amen. We whose names are underwritten, the loyal subjects of our dread sovereign Lord, King James, by the grace of God, having undertaken for the glory of God and the advancement of the Christian faith, and honor of our king and country, a voyage to plant the first colony in the northern parts of Virginia, do by these present solemnly and mutually in the presence of God, and one another, covenant and combine ourselves together.

Three hundred and thirty-four years later, Supreme Court Chief Justice Earl Warren stated: "I like to believe we are living today in the spirit of the Christian religion. I like also to believe that as long as we do so, no great harm can come to our country."

Even though there is historical evidence in favor of a religious government, common sense is still lacking. A first-grader's father (an atheist) tied up the court refusing to have his child cite the Pledge of Allegiance. A professional baseball team was forced to ban all signs brought into the stadium because John 3:16 contains a religious message. A little girl asked by school officials to sing a song in the winter (Christmas) pageant, was suddenly told her choice of music was inappropriate because the lyrics referred to the birth of Christ.

In Paul's second letter to Timothy (3:1-4) a not-so-subtle warning was given. "But understand this: there will be terrifying times in the last days. People will be self-centered and lovers of money, proud, haughty, abusive, disobedient to their parents, ungrateful, unreligious, callous, implacable, slanderous, licentious, brutal, hating what is good, traitors, reckless, conceited, lovers of pleasure rather than lovers of God."

I wonder what Paul would write today if he were told, "You are violating the First Amendment."

Danika

---

10 August

Dear Parent's Group:

It seems your topics are generating a great deal of discussion. Allow me to pose some additional questions you may want to deliberate.

ON YOUTH VIOLENCE: When was the last time the media didn't report a story about some child, adolescent or teenager involved in violence? When you were young, were violent acts as common as they are today? Vicious attacks involving younger and younger children strike fear into parents at all socioeconomic levels. Bad kids? Bad parents? Bad legislation? Symptoms? Yes. The real cause? No.

ON SEXUAL PROMISCUITY: If teenage sex has always been (and it always has), why the escalation in teenage pregnancies, sexually transmitted diseases, abortion, and AIDS? Are hormones more intense or is society more encouraging? If sex education is the solution, why are there more kids in trouble than there were a generation ago? How do you explain the tens of thousands of young people who have chosen abstinence? How many parents willingly endorse the teaching of masturbation, homosexuality, intercourse, and abortion to a child? Does this scenario sound appealing?

ON HOMOPHOBIA: What does this term really mean? Hatred for gay men and lesbian women, or fear of the moral consequences associated with their behavior? Is disapproval of the act discrimination or discernment? If society embraces the homosexual lifestyle can Sodom II be far behind?

ON CENSORSHIP: Should parents defend their child's right to seek unlimited pleasures? If censorship is against the law, then how do judges justify censoring criminals from their right to pursue happiness?

ON ABORTION: Ask young people how they would feel if their best friend had been aborted. Challenge sons and daughters to weigh the consequences of condemning the baby who one day may have found the cure for AIDS; brought a lasting peace to the planet; or led the fight to protect the environment. Don't stop there. Inquire as to how they would feel about the creation of a super race, destroying cradle-to-grave candidates who don't measure up. Tell them that if they are short, of average intelligence, artistically deficient, athletically imperfect, or a rung below beautiful, they may not qualify for existence. Remind them that if they were born with a genetic impairment, society may one day encourage the termination of their children. And, if their parents are judged to be a burden, the state may ask for authorization to destroy mom and dad. If sanctity of life is not the issue, what is?

ON SEPARATION OF CHURCH AND STATE: This country was founded by a religious people whose constitution was based on Judeo-Christian morality. Why then would a nation's best political and legal minds quarantine God from His people? Why should the demands of a few dictate how the masses may celebrate Christmas? Should a national youth organization with over 100 years of history be mandated to change their constitution because parents of one child are offended by a single word—God?

My dearest parents, I hope my questions will strengthen your resolve "To Face The Wind."

Paul, Town Elder

Chapter Five

If I Only Had A Brain

——— ✿ ———————————————————————————————————

I have come to a frightening conclusion that I am the decisive element in the classroom. . . . As a teacher, I possess tremendous power to make a child's life miserable or joyous. I can be a tool of torture or an instrument of inspiration. I can humiliate or humor, hurt and heal. In all situations, it is my response that decides whether a crisis will be escalated or de-escalated, and a child humanized or dehumanized.

—Dr. Hiam Ginott

Part I
To Reap What They Sow

If I could get to the highest place in Athens I would lift up my voice to say: What mean ye, fellow citizens, that ye turn every stone to scrape wealth together, and take so little care of your children, to whom ye must one day relinquish all?

—Socrates

———————————————————————————————————————

13 August

Dear Darcee and Danika:

Everything we see on television or read in the newspapers, suggests that the educational system has deteriorated. Teacher mediocrity, lower test scores, classroom violence, and a strategic retreat from the three R's, dominate the nightly news.

Are schools really failing, or are the problems blown out of proportion? And, if the problems are real, who's to blame? Educators? Parents? Or both?

John and Ronica

---

16 August

Dear John & Ronica:

Let me calm your fears. The public education system in this country is the best in the world. However, to expect that every schoolteacher is perfect is unrealistic. As in any business, there will be a few employees who tend to give the institution a bad name.

In my previous letters I have cautioned parents to avoid worrying about other kids. So too, with inferior schools and their teachers. As responsible parents you need not worry. Your children will not be adversely affected by other-side-of-the-track education.

The problem is not teacher based. Study after study points to apathetic mothers and fathers, resulting in too many incompetent parents who care less about their children's education. Obviously, the parents of Mir, Montana represent the majority of loving, caring guardians. But, there is also something else your group represents. Parents like John and Ronica are too busy to worry about day-to-day operations of a classroom.

Three children under seven years of age demand too much of your precious time. Both of you work. Both must take care of the home. Both of you are exhausted.

It is not fair to ask working parents to visit schools, attend PTA meetings, or volunteer for chauffeuring duties. Let stay-at-home moms take care of the details. They have plenty of energy to get involved.

There's another reason to keep your nose out of the education business. Today's teachers are professionals. Their job is to prepare your children for life. Teachers know what needs to be taught. They know what tools to use and how to use them. What they don't need is med-dling parents who never taught a day in the classroom.

Adversaries of public schools are constantly criticizing educators for not doing the job. If the kid gets bad grades, the teacher is at fault. If the subject conflicts with right-wing philosophies, administration is out of line. But, if the teacher strikes for a fair wage, lower class size, or tougher discipline policies, parents shirk their responsibilities by not supporting public education.

Added to these burdens are Christian coalition de-mands for school choice initiatives. These radicals are the same people who often lead a vote against needed school levies. They scream that teaching values is the jurisdiction of parents. Then they turn around and threaten to send their kids to private schools where children are brain-washed with religious dogma.

Parents worry that standards are dropping and tax dollars are wasted. What they forget is that troubled kids from bad neighborhoods, and/or bad parents, continually bring aggregate scores down. If society did not have to deal with these undesirables, American education would be the envy of the world.

So before you get an "F" for failing your public school system, get on the right track and support those teachers whose job it is to educate your children.

Darcee

---

16 August

Dear John & Ronica:

Parents who take education seriously are headed down the right path. There was a time when moms would load their little ones on the school bus, wave good-bye, and trust that their children would receive a quality education.

There was no talk of lowering standards, rising disci-pline problems, or teaching values. Parents didn't have to worry about report cards passing or failing the child's "self-esteem." Teachers loved to teach and parents loved to parent. The two worked together.

Those days are gone. Teachers excitedly count down the days when they can escape the classroom to a safe retirement. Many children are out of control and too few parents in control. School administrators spend the majority of their time trying to raise funds to avoid teacher strikes, and crumbling buildings. Meanwhile, federal and state bureaucracies continually demand one social experiment after another.

These problems are not unique to public schools in poor neighborhoods. All schools are affected. All children are vulnerable. All parents accountable. Before we pass judgment, let's see what happens when common sense and accountability give way to irrational behavior.

In a small East Coast town a teacher was fired because she gave too many F's and D's to her students. Parents, Administration, and School Board members challenged the math teacher to explain why she gave such low grades. Her response: "I just couldn't pass kids who were failing my Algebra course." Her defense failed, and after ten years of motivating high school students, the teacher was fired. But, then, a funny thing happened. The student body walked out of school wearing buttons and carrying signs which blamed themselves for failing Algebra. This professional was eventually vindicated and is again back where she belongs—the classroom.

A generation ago teachers who were tough were respected. Parents rarely complained to the principal. Administration would refuse to lower standards. Board members didn't lose their seats every election. And children who chose to blame teachers for their failures were fortunate to survive the wrath of parents.

Today's curriculum is decidedly easier. Students don't work as hard. Parents are less involved. Many teachers shun accountability. Teaching values is forbidden, as educators are encouraged to provide "value neutral" lesson plans. Ironically, everyone complains that youth lack self-control, often confusing right and wrong. Added to this are taxpayers who reject levy after levy because they don't understand why children can't read, write a sentence, or answer a simple math problem.

The answer to these problems often begins with school administration. Low fail ratios are endorsed. Children with violent behavior are passed on grade-to-grade, school-to-school. No one wants the troublemaker back. Many parents miss teacher meetings or fail to pick up report cards. Author Richard Louv quotes the frustrations of one high school teacher.

> School is a colossal bore to most kids and teachers. As a teacher you're isolated in the classroom and nobody comes in to help you improve. These administrators come in and take notes in the back of the room and observe you, but they're just going through the motions. Teachers work behind closed doors. They face these distracted, bored kids who are getting all their information from television. School gets out at two o'clock in the afternoon, and the kids can do whatever they want. They can go home and get laid or do drugs, or do nothing. What do the schools offer? Longer days and longer courses. But longer days and classes of what?

The bottom line is this: Are students prepared to become responsible adults? Have they learned their math? Can they write? Do they know how to solve complex problems? Is work ethic part of their vocabulary? Do they have strong character? Are they resourceful, self-disciplined? Will they be accountable for their actions? Have they learned to respect authority? Can they discern right from wrong? Does temperance mean anything to them?

The problems are real. All of us are responsible when we choose to demand less than the best from teachers, administrators, parents, and children.

The challenge is not simply to select a school and put a child on the bus. The challenge is to get involved. William A. Ward, 19th Century philosopher said it this way.

"Blessed is the person who sees the need, recognizes the responsibility and actively becomes the answer."

                                                            Danika

---

                                                    18 August
Dear Darcee and Danika:

Darcee appears to understand that parents generally have less time to get involved with schools. However, her "butt-out" advice is troubling. Danika calls for more parent activism. The questions are when and how? On a related topic, parents from our group are confused over the outcome-based education (OBE) controversy. Is this a positive step for public education or a motivator for home schooling?

                                                    John and Ronica

---

                                                    22 August
Dear John & Ronica:

I have read Danika's advice on parental involvement and have reached the conclusion that she is out of touch with education.

Danika criticizes parents for their indifference, then turns around and invites them to get involved. One thing teachers don't need are incompetent parents roaming the halls. Parents who stay out of class stay out of trouble.

Another objection is Danika's continued push for teaching values. Terms like "temperance" strongly suggest right-wing fundamentalism. Teaching of values belongs in the home—not the school.

Let's discuss outcome-based education. In its simplest form, OBE is a progressive way to level the playing field. No longer will the "class brain" grab all the honors. Gone are report card pressures which embarrass children who are not blessed with academic or environmental assets accorded their peers. Instead of worrying about a "B" on a meaningless test, students are challenged to understand and appreciate their worth as unique individuals. Academic nerds with low self-esteem will be rescued as OBE concentrates on emotions and feelings through a series of "learning outcomes."

Competition, honors, and letter grades traditionally favor the bright student. The OBE teacher will encourage children to do what's best for them. By improving the child's self-esteem, OBE will permit all students to feel good about themselves and what they accomplished. In Los Angeles, teachers have been told to "give top grades to students who mastered subjects expected of their grade level." Pennsylvania's State Board of Education has also recommended OBE. If a child does poorly on a test, they may take it again until the student earns an "S" grade, meaning area of strength. Even our nation's capital, Washington, D.C., has fallen in line as "F's" are no longer an approved letter grade.

Enthusiasm is spreading as administrators move to overhaul an ancient teaching system developed to satisfy colonial farmers. National adoption of OBE is expected. Don't miss the opportunity to publicly support OBE when it comes to your school.

One major OBE benefit is the diffusion of school choice initiatives. Proponents of choice falsely believe that parents who select the school they want their child to attend, will guarantee success for that child. Such nonsense is destructive. If parents are given vouchers to "buy" education, a system would develop where the buyer of the product is not qualified to discern good from bad, progressive from primitive. Mothers and fathers would respond to rumor, innuendo, and Madison Avenue advertising. Children could also be a hindrance as they push to attend the school where their friends go.

Voucher distribution would result in the formation of "elitist" schools open only to the academically gifted. The rest of the kids would be left out in the cold. Needed monies for local community schools would dissipate, eventually forcing an increase in taxes. Private schools would continue to prosper at the expense of public education.

Imagine a parent permitted to designate their tax defense dollars to the weapon of their choice. Our military would be severely weakened as Army, Navy, Marine, and Air Force advertising executives fight for citizen dollars. Given this scenario, how well would you sleep at night?

The same disastrous consequences await parents who dare to invest in the scholastic weapon of choice. Some parents will demand Magnet schools designed to maximize their child's potential. Others will opt for mandatory religious values, satisfying their fundamentalist appetites. The result will be chaos, bankruptcy, discrimination, and failure.

A related matter is home schooling. This choice is even more radical than Magnet school or voucher programs. Led by antiestablishment parents, home school advocates are control freaks.

Children taught at home miss the camaraderie of their friends. They are taught value laden material by unqualified teachers.

Home schooling is a dangerous step toward segregation. Children brainwashed by their parents represent a potential threat to the security of state-approved education. And, unless program content is monitored and home schoolers are screened for competency, an army of right-wing children will flood our communities.

Public education is the only choice. Parents who choose otherwise risk not only their children's future, but the future of their country.

Darcee

---

22 August

Dear John and Ronica:

May I begin by agreeing with Darcee, that parental involvement in schools is troubling. Where we differ is that she would prefer to exclude parents from what's taught in the classroom. I feel it's mandatory that moms and dads become actively involved in the education of their children—and that includes content!

There is no question that parents' schedules are grueling. With more single parents and fewer stay-at-home moms, time is at a premium. But, time spent monitoring the education of children is crucial.

Consider that SAT scores have dropped more than eighty points in the last twenty-five years. There are more than a half million school dropouts per year. The vocabulary of American children at the beginning of this decade was a full fifteen thousand words less than children attending school at the end of World War II. And, among developed nations, the USA has the highest rate of illiteracy in the world.

Such sobering trends have not gone unnoticed. A recent *Parenting* magazine poll found that 50 percent of parents are concerned about poor curricula, while 62 percent worry about low academic standards. Parental fears accelerate when children can't do simple math, find Chicago on a map, recall the name of a single Supreme Court Justice, or identify the century when our nation's Civil War was fought. Equally frustrating are reports that many schools are focusing their energies on sex education, self-esteem, values clarification, and untold numbers of social experiments.

How should parents get involved? Attend PTA/PTO meetings, run for the School Board, and review textbooks for what's being taught. Watch for nonacademic programs where content conflicts with the values you've taught your children. Weigh school alternatives. Pick the best school which matches your financial ability to pay with the standard of education you expect. Support teachers, particularly where discipline and work ethic issues need to be addressed. Stay current on educational trends to be sure your children are getting the best product for your money. And finally, network with other parents whose values, concerns, and commitment parallel your own.

I would now like to turn my attention to a discussion about outcome-based education (OBE). In one state, the Board of Education has proposed fifty-one "learning outcomes" as necessary to qualify children for a high school diploma.

Instead of passing certain units of English, math, social studies, etc., OBE will require students to appreciate their worth as unique and capable individuals. They must exhibit self-esteem and be able to apply the fundamentals of consumer behavior in order to manage resources for personal and family needs.

If your child can't read, add, or think, but is convinced he has self-worth, he passes! State approved attitude and behavior will replace grades and test assessments. Accountability will dissipate as children, teachers, and administrators avoid performance measurements in traditional subjects. Slower students will eventually catch up with brighter kids, as the latter are not encouraged to excel. And, should a child struggle in a particular subject, the teacher will be careful not to hurt the student's feelings, choosing instead to "dumb down" expected results.

This is OBE. And this is one reason why parents are demanding the freedom to choose the school which will best return their tax dollar investment. OBE, classroom violence, poor academic performance, and valueless curricula represent the reasons why school voucher initiatives are beginning to appear at the ballot box. These issues are also responsible for the tremendous growth in home schooling.

Compounding these problems are the number of schools flirting with bankruptcy. Ironically, state and federal education expenditures inversely relate to SAT performance. In George Will's article, "Educators Losing Battle To Mislead The Public," the columnist correctly points out that five states with the highest SAT scores rank 27th, 44th, 42nd, 51st, and 25th respectively in per pupil expenditures. Will also notes that in the last twenty years, there has been a 47 percent increase in public education budgets with a corresponding 7 percent decline in school enrollment and a thirty-five-point decline in SAT scores.

Evidence of a public education crisis is demonstrated in consumer demand for phonics reading kits. These kits are popular with home schoolers. The success for these programs is due to education's move away from phonics in favor of reading techniques which capitalize on picture-word association.

If choice will destroy the public education system, why then do so many public school teachers educate their children in private schools? Thousands of public school teachers in San Francisco, L.A., Chicago, New Orleans, Memphis, and multiple other cities have made the decision to give their children private school education. In Milwaukee, 50 percent of the teacher population has followed suit.

Maybe it's because the average private school scores 100 SAT points higher than the average public school. Perhaps it's because discipline is stricter, Judeo-Christian values are encouraged, and traditional pass/fail criteria are used to determine if the child knows the three R's. And, though private school teachers earn up to $10,000 less than their public counterparts, many trust the system.

Then again, maybe it's simply parental involvement. Teachers who are parents know exactly what must be done, and they're doing it. As parents, you have the responsibility to ensure your children get an education. With that responsibility comes the right to see that your choice is the best one possible.

Danika

Part II
Back to the Catacombs

The philosophy of the schoolroom in one generation will be the philosophy of government in the next.

—Abe Lincoln

25 August

Dear Darcee and Danika:

A major concern for me is whether values should be taught in the classroom.

Though it may be advantageous to reinforce moral principals, can parents be sure that their children will be exposed to the same values they learn at home?

Experts often refer to the classroom as the cultural battlefield. If so, to what degree do parents have a right to monitor, even control, what's taught to their children?

Vasya

28 August

Dear Vasya:

Wouldn't it be a wonderful world if all parents had the same values you do; if their kids epitomized the very morals you stressed with your children; if all teachers were cloned to ensure your morality was taught? If parents stay in the home and allow teachers to remain in the classroom, society can accomplish a simple moral philosophy. As it is, one group of parents will demand that a values course be part of a mandatory curriculum, while other parents sabotage school board meetings the minute anyone mentions values.

One teacher said it best: "They want us to teach values, they want us to teach a tougher curriculum, they want us to parent their children because they don't have time—and, 'oh, by the way, we're cutting your budget.'" "They" are parents.

Values represent a smoke screen for real issues. Sex education, New Age philosophies, sexism, suicide prevention, cultural diversity, health clinics, conflict resolution, character education, self-esteem training, and prayer in school are all hotbeds of controversy.

In many courses, parents are taught to avoid communication blocks between adult and teen. Examples include "moralizing," which serves only to remind teens that they can't choose their own values; "interrogating," which is nothing more than a cross examination designed to find fault; "advice giving," a humiliating process which reminds teens that they can't come up with their own solutions; and "commanding," which dares to communicate to the teen that he or she has no right to handle his or her problems.

If parents can't agree on how to parent at home, how can they possibly reach a consensus on whether sex education should be taught, values discussed, or health clinics be available at school?

Let the teachers teach. Let the administrators administer. And let the kids learn. Don't worry about textbooks—stick to cookbooks. Your role in the condom affair stops at your bedroom door—not the classroom door. And, while you're at it, pray for the school if you must, but only in a house of prayer, not a house of learning.

When moms and dads learn to be open-minded and nonjudgmental, the problems between teacher and parent will subside.

Fortunately, organizations like People For The American Way serve as a reminder of why parents must stay out of the way of the educational system. In the organization's fifteenth annual survey, entitled "Attacks On The Freedom To Learn," researchers found 376 incidents of parental attempts to censor public school materials.

Sadly, most of the controversy focused on enhancing a child's self-esteem.

Parents who refuse educators the right to improve children need not worry about what's taught at school; rather, they should worry about what they're teaching their kids at home!

Darcee

                                    28 August

Dear Vasya:

There is a cultural war taking place in our nation's classrooms. To capture the seriousness of the campaign, consider this passage from *Humanist* magazine:

> I am convinced that the battle for humankind's future must be waged and won in the public classroom . . . by teachers . . . who correctly perceive their role as proselytizers of a new faith; a religion of humanity . . . that recognizes and respects what theologians call the divinity of every human being. The classroom must and will become an arena of conflict between the old and the new—the rotting corpse of Christianity . . . and the new faith of Humanism. . . . It will undoubtedly be a long, arduous, painful struggle replete with much sorrow and many tears, but Humanism will emerge triumphant.

This secular battle cry must be silenced by parents who become actively involved in the education of their children.

Study after study has ranked parental involvement as a number one teacher need. The trick is to build an atmosphere of trust between parent and educator by reaching a consensus on moral standards best suited for the classroom environment.

The first order of business is to answer the question: "Whose standards should be used when teaching values in the classroom?" There are two answers to this tiring debate. First is common sense. Would any responsible parent or educator disagree with the teaching of honesty, compassion, self-discipline, or hard work? Is there an adult out there who would argue that young people should never learn to respect authority? Are not loyalty, traditions, patriotism, volunteerism, and a spiritual foundation, representative of our forefathers' character? When the "Spur

Posse" gang (high school boys accused of exploiting girls as a measure of sexual conquests) story broke, one member told a reporter: "They pass out condoms, teach sex education and pregnancy-this and pregnancy-that. But they don't teach us any rules." Is it not reasonable to assume that if that boy had been taught how to discern right from wrong, instead of how to apply a condom, the Spur Posse gang might have had one less member?

A second argument is based on five hundred years of history. When pilgrims hit the shores, they brought Judeo-Christian ethics with them. Succeeding generations would establish a constitutional roadmap from the same moral principles. Today, the highest court in the land begins its daily sessions with the words, "God save the U.S. and the Honorable court."

William J. Bennett, past Secretary of Education, has long been a proponent of values education. His position is clear. "What determines a young person's behavior in academics, sexual and social life, are his deeply held convictions and beliefs. They determine behavior far more than race, class, economic background, or ethnicity." Bennett goes on to say: "Nature abhors a vacuum. So does a child's soul. If that soul is not filled with noble sentiments, with virtue, if we do not attend to the better angels of our nature, it will be filled with something else. These matters are of overwhelming importance to our children."

Listen to Bennett's words. Then listen to your heart. You not only have a right to influence and control what your children learn in the classroom, but as parents, you have a duty to do so.

Remember the Crosby, Stills and Nash line, "teach your children well?" Long before their words, a Proverb warned: "Train up a child in the way he should go and when he is old he will not depart from it."

Danika

31 August

Dear Darcee and Danika:

Contrary to your recommendation, Darcee, it's clear that parents must play an active role in education.

Before we jump into the fray, however, please give us a better feel for the challenges parents will likely encounter in their quest for strengthening the academic and moral foundation of their children.

Vasya

---

3 September

Dear Vasya:

The question you must ask is whether you and your colleagues can handle the warning I'm about to give.

Since you've obviously chosen to ignore my counsel, then prepare to become embroiled in a win-less controversy which will undoubtedly affect the self-esteem of your children. If this is what you want, this is what you'll get.

Teachers, principals, and school board officials will label your meddling as inappropriate behavior. Your demand for a greater voice in classroom instruction will be seen as part of a right-wing fundamentalist agenda. Not only will you be branded a radical by administration, but also by other parents who see your activism as disruptive.

Likely, you'll get your day in court where you will be challenged by teachers schooled in nondirective teaching methods; research reports supportive of sex education programs; ACLU lawyers equipped to defend the First Amendment; psychologists who advocate sensitivity training, and parenting experts who remind you that conflict resolution must begin with parents' willingness to defer to the rights of their children. And, if you're real lucky, you may have the opportunity to look ridiculous before the cameras. If this happens, prepare to lose face and friends. Meanwhile, your kids will become a laughing stock in school, while their mother continues her "witch hunt" only to find she's after the wrong witch.

After you realize you can't win at the school level, you'll probably run for a seat on the school board, only to lose because of your fanatical behavior. You may even choose to say "no" to the school levy, hoping your protest vote will send a signal to administration. Unfortunately, you will only hurt the kids.

Perhaps you'll begin a campaign to get "school choice" on the ballot. Prepare for another setback as parents and teachers resoundingly defeat your initiative.

Finally, you may elect to get into the business of home schooling. As a single parent do you have the time? No! Do you have the training? No! Will your children be excited to lose their friends? No! Will they enjoy alienation from school sports and other organized activities? No! Be proud of their mother for making a fool of herself? No!

So, what's left? How about common sense? Not the kind Danika promotes as she encourages parents to rise up in revolt against an American institution. But the kind which demands restraint, especially in areas outside of parental authority.

Avoid the traps reserved for troublemakers whose ambition is fueled by accusations against authorities.

Ignore my advice and face the consequences. Come to your parental senses and reap the rewards. The choice is yours.

Darcee

---

3 September

Dear Vasya:

The first thing to remember is that parents who are concerned about moral education are in sync with America's population. In a recent poll, more than six out of ten adults clearly felt that the nation is experiencing a moral decline.

You're not alone. Many parents are concerned with the educational system. Though part of their anxiety is academic in nature, a significant cause for worry is focused on values, or the lack thereof.

All over the country children as young as ten are bringing questions home about anal and oral sex, suicide, rape, and a host of homework assignments challenging parental authority.

Adolescents are invited into moral scenarios by teachers forbidden to provide right or wrong responses.

Teenagers learn the consequences of promiscuity because abstinence is a "religious" term. These same young people are told they can't pray, read the Bible, or study the Ten Commandments; they can, however, attend a condom course, or study new age philosophies.

The school which chooses to resist moral teaching while encouraging independence from parental authority will:

1. Experience staggering teenage pregnancy rates.

2. Find that seven in ten boys will become sexually active before they leave high school.

3. Graduate more functionally illiterate children than any previous generation.

4. Lose up to one in four kids to high school dropout rosters.

5. Expose students to ever increasing violence, drugs, and other antisocial behavior.

6. Encourage diversity training with pro-homosexual curricula.

7. Continue to pass students who are ill-prepared for the world of work.

Jamie Escalante, the Los Angeles calculus teacher whose impressive story was told in the movie *Stand and Deliver*, totally ignored the public school mandate that a teacher shouldn't impose his values on students. Escalante's response: "My values are better than theirs." His students agreed and their mathematics performance far exceeded the national average.

James Michener wrote,

> As a young man I was taught to treat all races with justice. . . . I was taught that loyalty to one's nation was an obligation. . . . I was taught the good citizen pays his taxes, supports schools, libraries and museums. I was advised to cling to good people and shun the bad, and I have tried. I realize there are considerations and pressures for young people today that did not exist for me. . . . Yet the values I learned must endure and be taught—as the foundation for the America of tomorrow. They must be taught in the home, in religious training, in the Boy scouts and Girl Scouts, in Little League, in the media. And most critically, as a guarantee that everyone will be exposed to them, they must be taught in school.

Michener's last line is clear. VALUES MUST BE TAUGHT IN SCHOOL! This is your challenge. Don't be afraid to stand up for what you believe. If you choose not to impose your values on the educational system, that same system will impose its values on your children. If that happens, families will eventually retreat to the catacombs to avoid the evil of an immoral society.

Danika

Part III
Hi Ho, Hi Ho—
It's Off to Welfare We Go

One of the things my parents taught me was a work ethic. It was honorable to work. Work did not bring dignity to the individual, but the individual brought dignity to the work. Along with the work ethic went the principle of discipline and responsibility practiced by our family.

—Ken Wessner
Past Retired Chairman, Service Master

6 September

Dear Darcee and Danika:

It's been awhile since I've retired, but I remember the day the plant manager gave me my watch for forty years of service. I was proud to have my wife, Jan, our children and grandchildren present when my boss said that I embodied the work ethic.

I doubt whether most young people understand what a work ethic is. Jan and I have seen too many parents struggle with their children over chores around the home. We are amazed at the number of fast-food managers who have complained about employees who fail to show up for their assigned shifts or can't add up the customer's bill. Jan is especially irritated at children on our street who decline a job to mow our grass or shovel our snow.

What can parents and grandparents do to remind youth that work is a privilege?

Jan and Richard

9 September

Dear Jan and Richard:

I find it fascinating that so-called loving parents demand that their children experience manual labor. Get good grades; clean your rooms; don't watch TV; cut the grass; take care of your sister; help your dad. Where does it end? How will a kid grow up when his parents pile so many responsibilities on him? As an adolescent he is expected to do chores around the house, earn spending money from a part-time job, and still make the honor role. His sister must work, volunteer, and get into college.

When will these children be allowed to enjoy life? Isn't it the parents' responsibility to work? Must child labor laws be violated so young people have a chance to fulfill their life-style needs?

I can hear Richard mumbling something to the effect that "when he was a boy . . ." Fortunately, Richard, when you were a boy educational pressures were minimal, allowing more time to work around the farm. Youth had time to deliver papers, paint fences and cut the neighbor's lawn.

But times have changed. There's school, piano lessons, baseball practice, and prime-time TV. Kids don't have time to work. That privilege will come with adulthood.

I would suggest that parents and grandparents worry less about the "work ethic" and more about pleasing their children. Time devoted to making kids happy is time well spent. And should this include delivering papers with your son because he wants to earn a little extra money, then fine. If this necessitates bending curfews to allow your daughter to baby-sit, then good. You are giving the child the opportunity to choose work because he or she wants it; not because some adult feels kids must work. A strong work ethic begins at work. This is at the very heart of the Protestant work ethic. Besides, if parents are successful, their children will have it much easier in life. And isn't this what all parents want for their kids? In fact, isn't this what you want for your grandchildren?

Darcee

---

9 September

Dear Jan and Richard:

A child's work ethic begins at home. When children learn that family members must help maintain the home, they become contributing members of that family. As children work hard in school they learn the values of initiative and resourcefulness. Parents who teach their children to give "back" to the community, have a better chance of raising productive members of society. Kids who are part of a team quickly recognize the spirit of working together to achieve a common goal. Young people who work hard intuitively understand the value of monetary reward for a job well done. And a strong work ethic will come in handy for any boy or girl who chooses to personally develop his or her God-given talents.

Lack of a work ethic is too often identified with the workforce. In a national survey, 78 percent of respondents believed that low productivity was a direct result of changing work attitudes. Instead of hard work, four out of ten workers freely admitted that "leisure" was the most important thing in life. Forty-five percent of college students agreed as they put relaxation ahead of work.

But a poor work ethic also reaches down to the classroom. In another survey, high school principals and small business owners concurred that today's high school graduates have poor math skills, abysmal writing skills, and weak listening skills.

Before parents of academically superior children turn a deaf ear, consider that many valedictorians who graduate from public and private schools exhibit only average achievement in the workforce. The message . . . brains do not guarantee a strong work ethic.

Has the younger generation sworn off work? The answer is yes and no. Children emulate the actions of their parents. If mom and dad work hard on the job, in the home, and for the community, children notice. If children are expected to clean their rooms, pick up their toys, clean the table and do their share of household chores, they learn responsibility. If young people know that their academic performance must meet certain standards, they learn accountability.

If parents fail to send a strong message, they can anticipate that their children will lack the necessary character and attitude needed to survive in the world of work.

Children must be made to understand that should they ignore the resources available to them (educators, parents, homework, etc.) then they are accountable for the consequences associated with such behavior.

Another challenge is parents are often victims of their own generosity. In a recent conversation with a second grade boy about chores he could do at home, he was overheard to say, "The maid cleans everything, even my room, so there's nothing I need do."

This boy's mom and dad, blessed with an income to afford such a service, have, in effect, done their son a terrible disservice. Without the privilege of work he has no work ethic. Added to this is the abundance of material gifts thrown his way. Unless he works hard and develops the character needed to be successful, he has little chance of maximizing his potential. Thomas Jefferson said, "Material abundance without character is the surest way to destruction." Chuck Colson and Jack Eckerd, authors of *Why America Doesn't Work* gives parents and grandparents ten two-letter words worth noting. "If it is to be, it is up to me."

Danika

---

12 September

Dear Darcee and Danika:

Kids who choose not to work hard at school, home, or in the community, have far too much time on their hands. We feel this can lead to trouble.

Whoever said "the devil fills idle hands" must have been thinking about this generation of youth.

Speaking of generations, would both of you please educate us on the "X generation." What is it? Should parents and grandparents be concerned?

Jan and Richard

---

15 September

Dear Jan and Richard:

Perhaps you missed the main point of my letter. KIDS DON'T HAVE TIME TO WORRY ABOUT THE WORK

ETHIC! They are too busy trying to enjoy childhood. Work can wait.

Parents and grandparents must allow children to find their own way. The only role adults may legitimately fill is banker, offering financial support necessary to allow young people the opportunity to enjoy life. Kids are not stupid. They know how much studying they should do. They can pick extracurricular activities without parental interference. They understand what, if any, chores they can take on around the house. And, believe it or not, they know what will make them happy.

These ten little words say it better than I, "If it is to be, it is up to me." Where in these words of wisdom are parents or grandparents invited? Those with too much time on their hands are victims of overprotective parents or meddling grandparents.

Before I discuss Generation X, I need to refute Danika's nonsense. According to her, children who have a strong work ethic probably have had hardworking parents. Well, I'm sorry, but there are thousands of stories about successful people who grew up with lazy parents or no parents at all. There are also thousands of teachers who will tell you how surprised they were to learn that the lazy, good-for-nothing student is now a respected citizen in the community. The bottom line is that work ethic will be developed from within. Kids will mature as needed without intrusion by parents. And children who do fail, will, in more cases than not, be a by-product of a society that has let them down.

This brings me to Generation X. The label applies to "twenty-something" adults who worked hard in high school and college only to discover that their life-style dreams may never be realized.

Young people were promised that a career opportunity would follow graduation. They were promised that they could be anything they wanted to be, earn as much as they want, and own whatever pleases them.

Instead of success, many graduates with master degrees are earning $5.00 per hour in fast-food restaurants. These young adults are forced to live with their parents until something comes along more befitting their needs and desires.

Newsweek guest columnist, Daniel Smith-Rowsey, in his article "The Terrible Twenties" has this warning for parents. "If there's any part of you left that still loves us enough to help us, we could really use it. And it's not just your last chance. It's our only one."

My comments put the blame for Generation X's troubles squarely on the shoulders of adults who promised that hard work has its rewards. All the more reason for your kids to carve out their own future.

Darcee

---

15 September

Dear Jan and Richard:

Generation X youth are often frustrated. This segment of society is quickly learning that to achieve their parents' standard of living will take a lifetime of work.

This is the same group who grew up on TV violence, psychotic movies, free-flowing profanity, sexually explicit rock lyrics and promises of instant gratification from drinking, drugs, and sex.

Some never worked, choosing instead to live off parents who willingly allowed their children to "milk" the system.

Generation X values often fail to discern good from evil. Their moral confusion is illustrated in a national poll of high school and college students. Almost two-thirds cheated on an exam in the last year. Sixteen percent said they have lied on a job application or resume and one-third of all students said they would do so in the future. Sadly, the incidence of lying, cheating and stealing was greater with high school students than their college counterparts.

In a related study, seven out of ten adults expect more instances of lying, cheating, and stealing in the future.

Author Richard Louv gives a chilling commentary by a high school student. When asked what his number one fear was, the student stated, "Kids." His reason: "Because kids will keep getting worse."

In another interview, Louv heard this remark. "If you have the type of parents that's always doing things for you, then when you do come of age, you will never want to take on that responsibility."

Together, these two young people have painted a portrait of a disillusioned generation, which one day will be responsible for the survival of this country. A cultural shock awaits the graduate who never learned the value of hard work. With this reality comes underemployment, welfare, or crime.

For employers, remaining competitive will become increasingly difficult as a generation of workers will emerge who fail to understand that character "is what you do when no one's looking." Instant gratification will represent the sum total of the new work ethic. Management will soon discover that the three R's and their cousin—critical thinking skills—are sorely lacking.

Authors Chuck Colson and Jack Eckerd relate what James Sheehy (a computer firm executive) feels about the expectations and psyche of younger employees. According to Sheehy, we have a new generation of workers whose "habits and experiences will plague future employers for years." Sheehy goes on to say, "Get ready America. There's more of this to come from the work force of tomorrow."

This is the world of Generation X. The challenge for some parents will be to make sure that Generations Y and Z do not follow older brothers and sisters whose work ethic is of little value, and in may cases, immoral. Said another way, remember what St. Augustine wrote: "Laborare est orare." To work is to pray.

Danika

Part IV
Condoms, Cucumbers, and Counseling

There's more of a stress on sex being so important in life. Since ninth grade, it's just been sex, sex, sex. Sex is constantly thrown at us.

—Interview by Richard Louv
with an 11th grade girl from his book,
Childhood's Future

---

18 September

Dear Darcee and Danika:

We realize that in previous correspondence to Vasya and Gillie you have touched upon the ever-increasing sexual activity of youth. The purpose of our letter is not to ask why virtue is fading, but rather, to inquire why it must be stolen from our children?

Said another way, what gives our schools the authority to teach our children about "the facts of life?"

Brina and Hasheem

---

21 September

Dear Brina and Hasheem:

"What gives our schools the authority to TEACH our children about the facts of life?" You answered your own question. Which institution is responsible for education? Schools. What is the responsibility of the teacher? To prepare your children to face the world! And, which environment best stimulates excited hands to be raised during a sex education session, or witness the sexual anxiety of young people who thirst for answers? The classroom!

But don't listen to me. Listen to the past Surgeon General of the United States. "I tell every girl that when she goes out on a date—put a condom in her purse." This statement from the leading health care authority should be reason enough to trust the education system.

As one Planned Parenthood executive says, "Kids are hungry for accurate information. They don't want to be moralized to."

No wonder school officials are pushing sex education. Kids need straight answers, as they are going to do what pleases them—not what pleases their parents. And moms and dads should quit worrying about adolescent behavior. As authors Lawrence Steinberg and Ann Levine state, "The reason your adolescent is questioning your judgement and engaging you in endless, tiresome debate is that she is maturing intellectually. She recognizes flaws in your logic and inconsistencies in your principles, and delights in pointing these out."

For further credibility consider that members of the National Guidelines Task Force on Sexuality Education believe that all youth must receive comprehensive sexuality education.

As reported in the booklet, *Guidelines for Comprehensive Sexuality Education Kindergarten Through Twelfth Grade,* "The primary goal of sexual education is the promotion of sexual health." The report goes on to say, "Sexuality education seeks to assist children in understanding a positive view of sexuality, provide them with information and skills about taking care of their sexual health, and help them acquire skills to make decisions now and in the future."

This is education we're talking about. These are experts who are doing the talking. Would a mother double the dosage the pediatrician recommends for her sick child? Would a father refute the advice the child's coach gives?

Simply put, stick to parenting and let educators focus on education.

Darcee

---

21 September

Dear Brina and Hasheem:

There are officials in government and school administration who believe that the classroom is the ideal place for providing sex education to children. Unfortunately, their enthusiasm for preparing students rarely includes the consequences associated with such behavior.

William Bennett's now famous cultural indicators include staggering increases in the percent of illegitimate births. In 1960, 5.3 percent of all babies were born out of wedlock. In 1992 that number jumped to 26.2 percent.

On a daily basis, over eight thousand teens contract a sexually transmitted disease, with gonorrhea infecting seventy-one thousand teenage girls. But how many of these same young ladies really wanted to have sex? A recent study of one thousand sexually active girls showed that their greatest need was HOW TO SAY NO!

Abstinence. Virtue. Shame. Fidelity. Temperance. Respect. These are the messages our youth are seeking. But, intimacy, condoms, masturbation, and oral sex are the lessons of the day.

In one city where condom education was the norm, pregnancies increased 31 percent. In a similar size city where abstinence was the focus, teenage pregnancy dropped 86 percent. Coincidence? Luck? I think not. Ask Dr. Malcom Potts, one of the inventors of condoms and president of Family Health International. Dr. Potts states, "Telling a person who engages in high-risk behavior to use a condom is like telling someone who is driving drunk to use a seat belt."

So-called "experts" fuel the push for school-based sex education with wild accusations that all teens are eventually "gonna do it"; therefore, let's show these kids how to do it right! The Executive Director of SIECUS (Sex Information and Education Council for the United States), the organization pushing mandatory sex education in schools, states in SIECUS Report 17, No. 1, "Safe Sex and Teens," that she and her colleagues have "fantasized about a national petting project to teach teenagers the techniques of petting, ranging from talking to flirting, dancing, hugging, kissing, necking, massaging, caressing, undressing each other, masturbation—alone or in groups."

The sex education manual, *Comfort, Confidence, Competence in Sexuality Education*, states that by age five the child should "understand the concept that a woman does not have to have babies unless she wants to, know where babies come from, how they 'get in' and 'get out,' and be able to talk about body parts without a sense of 'naughtiness.' "

And, if this isn't enough, the manual makes a claim that, "Only a small percentage (4-6%) of Americans are exclusively heterosexual or exclusively homosexual." This suggests that over 90 percent of the public are bisexual!

With garbage like this, it's no wonder that parents are beginning to irritate educators and politicians. And, it's not surprising girls willingly have sex with gang members as a rite of initiation; or "whirlpooling," where a gang of boys surround girls in city swimming pools, fondle and pull off swimsuits, is commonplace.

One boy who participated in whirlpooling said: "It's nature. Look at a female dog and a male dog. It's the same thing. You see twenty male dogs on a female dog. It's the male nature in a way."

A few years ago, not one of eight hundred sexologists attending an international conference raised their hand when a colleague asked audience members if they would have sex with the AIDS infected partner of their dreams if they had to rely on a condom for protection.

As parents, the choice is either to fight immorality or accept curricula like "Learning About Sex," which advises sadomasochism may be very acceptable and safe for sexual partners who know each other's needs. The author, Gary Kelly, further states, "A fair percentage of people probably have some sort of sexual contact with an animal during their lifetimes," and that there "are no indications that such animal contact are harmful."

Don Feder, syndicated columnist, makes this prediction. "Across the nation, parents are rising up, shouting, 'Not with my children you don't!' Their outcry will be heard from the halls of Congress to school committee elections."

I pray you and the parents of Mir, Montana have the courage to say, "Not with our children, you don't!"

Danika

---

24 September

Dear Darcee and Danika:

Our question is whether aggressive parental behavior is appropriate in the area of cultural diversity. Would parents be insensitive to others if they dared to put their moral position ahead of the feelings of others?

Brina and Hasheem

---

27 September

Dear Brina & Hasheem:

Neither of you should worry about insensitivity. You are the type of parents who scoff at the phrase "cultural diversity." It doesn't matter if minorities are subjected to bias-testing favoring Anglo-Saxon males. Parents who think like you willingly accept religion in the classroom without considering the feelings of other children who are forced to bow their heads to a God they don't believe in. And, if you had your way, gays and lesbians would be banned from your children's vocabulary.

Frankly, it wouldn't surprise me if you were to deny the dangers of sexual harassment or even discrimination.

Cultural diversity is being sensitive to the desires of others. Hopefully, your children will outgrow the sins of their parents.

Darcee

---

27 September

Dear Brina & Hasheem:

Cultural diversity is one of those "in" phrases which has been twisted to mean, "tolerance of any person or group's behavior," regardless of the consequences. There's no doubt that differing cultures may represent varying races, religions, or environmental customs. And, to respect these people is consistent with love of one's neighbor.

However, such differences should not include deviant behavior. Objections by a few should be overruled in favor of community standards. Sensitivity blown out of proportion should not be tolerated.

Let me give you some examples. In New York City, a teacher was found to be actively involved with NAMBLA (the North American Man/Boy Love Association) whose goal is the legalization of consensual sex between men and young boys. Because the teacher had not propositioned any student, some authorities believed he was entitled to keep his job. Others felt that his support for man/boy love philosophies was inappropriate.

As a parent, what do you think? Would you want your son taught by a man who belongs to an organization which supports pedophilia? Would it be insensitive to prohibit a pyromaniac to work in a fireworks factory? Is a beer distributor wrong for refusing an alcoholic a job? Are Boy Scout executives out of line when they refuse to allow homosexual males scout leadership positions? Are parents insensitive when they expect teachers to pass competency exams?

Would moms and dads be unfair if they objected to the teaching of the gay and lesbian lifestyle to children who are unprepared to understand their own sexuality, let alone the perversion of others?

Why should parents approve the teaching of immoral behavior in one classroom and the rejection of school prayer in another? When a child is pushed by her father to object to a "moment of silence" at a graduation ceremony, is such action not insensitive to the needs of her fellow students?

Supporters of the sensitivity movement often solidify their position under the harassment banner. Young people, grade school to college, are now being warned to avoid unwelcome advances, words or looks that could be judged inappropriate.

On the surface, educating students how not to offend the opposite sex has its merits. But, a closer look will reveal the dangers of pushing the harassment needle too far. In Wisconsin, high school students are exposed to a play entitled, "Alice in Sexual Assault Land." And, in Indiana, a teacher reported a six-year-old boy for kissing the top of the head of a little girl. The teacher claimed sexual harassment. The little girl never complained.

Parents must speak up even if someone is offended. Better to offend a few than to lose your children. Cal Thomas, syndicated columnist, states, "Professional educators and cultural manipulators see the minds, and increasingly the bodies and morals of our children as their exclusive property to be propagandized and manipulated as effectively as educators once did in the former Soviet Union."

The choice is simple. Morality or diversity? As parents, you have the right to decide.

Danika

Part V
Forbidden Fruit

The fruit of that forbidden tree, whose mortal taste brought death into the world, and all our woe.
—John Milton: *Paradise Lost I*

---

30 September

Dear Darcee and Danika:

Though my children are several years away from high school, I can't help but wonder what their classrooms will be like in the future. Gangs, drugs, violence . . . could it be worse?

Will our youth be expected to pass metal detectors as a prerequisite of coursework? Can I expect my children to announce that school authorities have affirmed the

student's rights to ignore his parents? And will such proc-
lamations carry over into college?

Please prepare this parent so I can prepare my children.

                                                        Gillie

---

                                              3 October

Dear Gillie:

Let's eliminate your fears. Typical school violence you
read about or see on network news is a product of bad
neighborhoods and bad parents. You live in Mir, Montana. You're a good parent. Why worry? Teachers you've
trusted will continue to pass your kids to other good teachers in other good schools.

As young ones mature in both academic and social
skills, the need for constant monitoring will decrease. Parent conference attendance will be optional. Strict curfews
will dissipate. Dress and music audits will give way to "growing up" needs of your adolescent.

Questions on friendships, dating, jobs, education, sex,
etc., will be replaced by stylish dress, material blessings,
car keys and unlimited trust.

Adolescent/teen maturity will blossom into man/wom-
anhood. And throughout the journey, authorities will provide appropriate counsel to your children. Educational
experts will see that your son and daughter are well experienced in independent thinking. By the time students are
ready to enter 9th grade, respect for the diversity of others will be second nature. And appreciation for their sexuality is guaranteed as sex education courses and condom
distribution programs are in every school in America.

When your children are ready for college they will
exercise their rights by choosing their career path, picking their partners, and worshiping their gods.

Parents who force their values on their kids will find
themselves in family divorce court. And adults who at-

tempt to restrict the child's right to choose will learn the consequences of First Amendment heresy.

When the next generation takes over the courts, industries, educational systems and political bureaucracies, inner city violence will curb as wealth redistribution and "victim" tolerance levels are heightened. Free drugs will eradicate the underworld. Sexual permissiveness will reduce violent attacks against women. And equal rights for all classes of citizens, regardless of sexual orientation, will be mandated.

These changes make for a better world. And thanks to your "letting go," your children will be responsible for a safer, freer society.

Your kids will thank you. Your grandkids will thank you. And I will thank you.

Darcee

---

3 October

Dear Gillie:

Parents must realize that the epidemic of youth violence in our schools is not the sole property of poorer neighborhoods. "One third of teachers feel that because of violence or the threat of violence their peers and the students in their school are less eager to go to school." In Chicago schools alone, there are 700 security guards patrolling the hallways. In 1965, Chicago had not a single guard on the payroll. Other school systems have purchased hand-held metal detectors to scan students for guns and knives. Some schools install expensive walk-through units. Reports of attempted teacher poisonings, stabbings, and shootings are beginning to surface in middle class America. In a small New England town, a high school junior stabbed and killed a man over a packet of cigarettes. The judge ruled that the young man may continue attending classes pending sentencing!

Sadly, too many parents assume random violence will never touch their community, school, or child. What they forget is that violence, like drugs, is not marketed by zip code. Children who commit crimes in other neighborhoods will eventually branch out touching, and in some cases, destroying distant lives. Drugs will proliferate; gang membership will grow; sexual attacks will be commonplace; even playground disagreements may turn into a bloodbath with one child viciously maiming another.

As the Ten Commandments are ripped from classroom walls, new literature will appear. Access to contraceptives, abortion counseling and clinic transportation free of parental interference, will be widely available.

The college years are not immune. Many higher learning institutions celebrate "condom distribution month." At one west coast college your son or daughter may acquire the Safe Sex Explorer's Action-Packed Starter Kit Handbook. Three thousand miles eastward, students at one Ivy League school may attend administration sanctioned condom races. At still another university, incoming freshman are advised that they may not object to a roommate because of his or her sexual orientation.

The future will not be pretty. Parenting will be a challenge for even the best. But unless moms and dads choose to meet that challenge, crimes against humanity will multiply.

Before you resign and turn your son or daughter over to local authorities, turn them over to God. Only then can you hope to win the fight for your children's souls.

                                                    Danika

---

                                    6 October
Dear Darcee and Danika:

One final question. I have heard that many nations have signed a resolution affirming the rights of children. What exactly does this action imply? And what impact will it have on kids?

                                                    Gillie

8 October

Dear Gillie:

I'm proud to be the one to inform you that the Children's Rights Treaty has been adopted by the international community. There is no better example of all that I've been preaching than that which protects the rights of children—regardless of parental meddling.

Fasten your seatbelt—for I'm about to let you listen in on the United Nations General Assembly's Convention on the Rights of the Child. Following is the "spirit" of the convention:

Article 1: A child is defined as any human being under the age of 18.

Article 2: No discrimination allowed.

Article 3: The best interests of the child shall be the primary consideration. The state has the final responsibility to ensure the child is protected.

Article 4: The state shall undertake all appropriate legislative, administrative and other measures for the implementation of the child's rights.

Article 8: The child has a right to his or her identity.

Article 9: The state shall ensure that a child shall not be separated from his or her parents against their will, EXCEPT when competent authorities find that separation is necessary for the best interests of the child.

Article 12: The state shall protect the right of the child to express his or her views freely in all matters affecting the child. Therefore, the child shall in particular be provided the opportunity to directly, or through an appropriate body, be afforded the right to be heard in judicial or administrative settings.

Article 13: The child shall have the right to freedom of expression; this right shall include freedom to seek, receive and impart information and ideas of all kinds, regardless of frontiers, either orally, in writing, or in print, in the form of art or through any other media of the child's choice.

Article 14: The state shall respect the right of the child to freedom of thought, conscience and religion.

Article 15: The state shall recognize the rights of the child to freedom of association and to freedom of peaceful assembly.

Article 16: No child shall be subjected to arbitrary or unlawful interference with his or her privacy.

Article 17: The state shall recognize the important function performed by the mass media and shall ensure that the child has access to information and material from a diversity of sources.

Article 19: The state will protect the child from all forms of abuse.

Article 20: The state shall protect the child from his or her family environment when the child's best interests are entitled to special protection and assistance from the state.

Article 21: Adoption shall be permitted to ensure the best interests of the child. Competent authorities shall authorize the state's decision.

Article 24: The state recognizes the child's right to the enjoyment of the highest attainable standard of health. As such, no child should be deprived of his or her right of access to such health care services. The state shall take all effective and appropriate measures with a view to abolishing traditional practices prejudicial to the health of children.

Article 27: The state recognizes the child's right to a standard of living adequate for the child's physical, mental, spiritual, moral, and social development.

Article 28: The state recognizes the right of the child to education.

Article 29: The state agrees that the education of the child shall be directed to: achieve the child's fullest potential; respect human rights and fundamental freedoms; respect the child's parents, cultural identity, language and values; tolerance for others; respect for the environment.

Article 30: Minority children may practice their own culture.

Article 32: Children may not be exploited for economic gain, and this includes performing any work that is likely to be hazardous or to interfere with the child's education, or to be harmful to the child's health, or physical, mental, spiritual, moral, or social development.

Article 36: The state shall protect children against all forms of exploitation prejudicial to any aspects of the child's welfare.

Article 37: No child shall be subjected to cruel and inhuman punishment. Neither capital punishment nor life imprisonment shall be imposed on children below eighteen years of age.

Article 39: The state shall be responsible for ensuring that all appropriate measures are taken to promote physical and psychological recovery and social re-integration of those children who are victims of neglect, exploitation, or abuse.

Article 40: Every child is presumed innocent until proven guilty according to the law.

Gillie, I trust you have come to your senses and realize that parenting experts from around the world are adamant about protecting the rights of the child. And, lest you think your government will allow parents to interfere, let me leave you and all Mir, Montana, with Article VI of the U.S. Constitution.

"This constitution and the laws of the United States which shall be made in pursuance thereof; and all treaties made, or which shall be made, under the authority of the United States, shall be the supreme law of the land; and the judges in every state shall be bound thereby, anything in the constitution or laws of any state to the contrary notwithstanding."

The day is coming when it will be against the law to disobey the United Nations General Assembly Convention on the Rights of the Child. And, when that day comes, children will be free.

Darcee

8 October

Dear Gillie:

No doubt Darcee strongly supports the United Nations Convention on the Rights of the Child. This seemingly innocent treaty could eventually regulate how parents raise their children. Written primarily to protect children from third world exploitations, the treaty's articles potentially open a pandora's box for parents.

Article 12 allows the child to express his or her own views freely in all matters. Does this suggest that immoral propaganda be allowed in your home?

Article 13 allows children to receive information of all kinds through "media of the child's choice." Does this mean unlimited access to every foul television program, record, or movie produced?

Article 14 states children shall have the freedom to choose the religion they want. Will parents still have the authority to bring their children up on the moral teachings of the church or synagogue of their choice?

Article 15 encourages "freedom of association." Will this law prohibit parents from banning their children from joining the KKK or other hate groups?

Article 16 protects the child's privacy. Abortion is a given. But, does it also mean that parents will be forbidden to search their child's room for material harmful to the child's health or moral development?

Article 17 guarantees the child's "access to the media." Prepare for state parenthood courtesy of cable TV.

Article 28 ensures that the child has a right to an education and that this process shall be compulsory and free to all. If the state controls what is taught and who will teach it, what authority will private schools have?

Article 37 guarantees every child free legal counsel. Such entitlements will surely burden the courts with parental divorce cases.

Gillie, though the proposed treaty may have good intentions, such language invites chaos in the family. If not carefully monitored, parents will end up partaking of a "new tree of knowledge." Only this time, it won't be paradise lost. It will be children.

Danika

---

11 October

Dear Paul:

This is my last correspondence. My final advice is above reproach.

1. Family values are guidelines—nothing more.

2. Traditional families represent a "state of mind" for old-fashioned parents who fear change.

3. Children have rights.

4. "Letting go" of childhood is an absolute.

5. Kids who are victims are *never* responsible for their behavior.

6. Entertainment in any form is in the eye of the beholder.

7. To deny a child's constitutional right to information or role models is censorship.

8. Youth violence is blown out of proportion.

9. Bad parents raise bad children.

10. Homophobia is wrong.

11. Controlled drug legalization may put an end to a war which has already been lost.

12. Parents who refute abortion, euthanasia, cloning and fetal transplants are censoring truth.

13. Educating children belongs in the classroom, not the family room.

14. "Values" have no place in school.

15. Today's students have little time to worry about a work ethic.

16. Educators are best qualified to teach sex education courses.

17. Tolerance for the diversity of others is more important than parental moralizing.

18. The Convention on the Rights of the Child will eliminate parental meddling.

Paul, I now have some advice for you. The next time you wish to recruit an expert on the science of raising children, don't hire a misguided fundamentalist whose agenda will destroy the state-child relationship. Remember, if the state is responsible for investing in its citizens, then it follows that such authority extends to children. As Marian Wright Adelman, head of the Children's Defense Fund warns, "our children are either going to be invested in or they're going to shoot at us."

When the children of Mir, Montana, start shooting, don't come running to me!

Darcee

---

12 October

Dear Paul:

Allow me to thank you and the parents of Mir, Montana, for giving me the privilege to serve. Hopefully, my counsel helped prepare these guardians for the crusade ahead. The following summarizes those positions which will help protect the souls of our children.

1. Going back to the fifties is not the answer. Going back to morals is.

2. Vigilance is *mandatory!*

3. Trust Him whom the prophets trusted.

4. Give your children limits.

5. *Freedom is just another word for everything to lose.*

6. Common ground does not mean compromise. Stand firm.

7. Hollywood, TV, and news media elite *do not* represent America.

8. Parents have the right, the obligation, and the moral duty to raise children according to God's laws.

9. Rock and rap lyrics should not be protected by the First Amendment.

10. Hell has heroes. Unless parents recognize them, many children will suffer.

11. Young people are searching for the courage to say, "No."

12. Homosexuality is immoral.

13. Censorship is a right of every parent.

14. Legalization of drugs, like passing out condoms, ignores moral accountability.

15. Parents *must* educate their children on the "sanctity of life."

16. Parents must teach that work is both a privilege and responsibility.

17. Parents who choose not to impose their values on the educational system, will find the same system imposing its values on their children.

18. Parents must invalidate the "Rights of the Child" treaty.

My assignment is finished. Before I go, let me share this final thought from a Connecticut father. "The single most important thing I'd write in a child-rearing book, chapter one, page one, first paragraph, is that you get back from parenthood what you put in."

I pray that the parents of Mir, Montana "reap what they sow."

Danika

---

14 October

Dear Parents' Group:

Following are some final questions the association may wish to ponder.

ON DECLINING EDUCATIONAL STANDARDS: Can parents really "turn the other cheek" and pretend schools are as good or better than the ones of a previous generation? And, if it's only bad neighborhoods which produce bad schools, why all the suburban violence, DARE programs, and "choice" initiatives? Is it possible that one

reason for so many school problems, is the state's development of young people? Is Outcome Based Education
the new standard for enhancing the self-esteem of children, or just another social experiment?

ON THE WORK ETHIC: If work ethic, as Darcee claims,
begins at work, how do you explain the differences in
academic, athletic or artistic performance among equally
capable youngsters? Aren't "Generation X" job applicants
a likely commercial for a society dangerously close to losing its work ethic?

ON TEACHING VALUES IN SCHOOL: Given the
choice, would you rather have your children memorize
The Ten Commandments, or how to put a condom on?
Consider the consequences of not standing up for children too young to stand up for themselves.

ON CULTURAL DIVERSITY: Why do educators, politicians, and the courts accept minority demands for teaching English as a second language; approve hate groups'
right to bring trouble to a community; endorse sexual
perversion—even against children? Doesn't such folly refute five hundred years of our nation's history?

ON DRUGS AND VIOLENCE IN SCHOOLS: If good
parents and their communities need not worry about the
safety of their schools, then why is fear on the minds and
in the hearts of every good mom and dad in America?

ON THE "CHILDREN'S RIGHTS" TREATY: Is it too
late for parents and their children? Is all we've discussed
for naught? Will parents have the courage to defend their
God-given right to raise their children?

My dearest parents, over the past several months Jan,
Richard, John, Ronica, Gillie, Brina, Hasheem, and Vasya
have represented your association well.

Your spokespersons developed the wisdom to discern
the human from the divine, good from evil. Today's dangers are real. And now, the United Nations General
Assembly's Convention on the Rights of the Child may
further drive a wedge between parents and their children.

It's easy to sound defeat. But the family has not lost! Yesterday I received an anonymous letter in the mail. As you read Parental Desiderate, allow me to leave you with a final thought by one of today's highly respected religious leaders, Billy Graham.

"I don't know what the future holds, but I know who holds the future."

Paul, Town Elder

Epilogue

Parental Desiderate

Parents are God's first line of defense. Your responsibility is awesome; your reward eternal. From tired babies to teens who never tire, you seldom rest. Your character is built to withstand disappointment, embarrassment, and sadness. Each will surely surface. Learn to confront rather than compromise. But, when it's your fault, say so. Only then will you experience a child's ability to forgive. Affection must overcome cynicism. Material gifts must give way to time, for the latter creates memories. Avoid humanistic terms of endearment; entitlements, victimology, diversity, and self-esteem only weave a tapestry of despair.

Abstain from truth debates. Good and evil were established long ago. Admonish your children that sex outside of marriage at any age with anyone of any sex, is wrong; free speech does not include vulgarity; violence is not a rite of passage; but discipline by hand or deed, is a parent's God-given right. Stem the tide for the "right" to choose alcohol, drugs, abortion or homosexuality. For such only serve to destroy a generation. Speak of values, morals, the Ten Commandments. Let these tenets magnify your freedom of expression.

Give your children the privilege of work, lest the future have no future. Censor evil, not God. A child raised without a spiritual foundation will surely crumble. Remember, freedom of speech is a gift. Use it. Educate your soul. Verbalize your morality condemning all immorality. Give your sons and daughters timeless heroes, not fleeting athletes, entertainers, or politicians whose message is self-serving. Trust the teacher, policeman, coach, clergy, or neighbor who lives a moral life. Never ignore the loving gifts and needs of the elderly. They have much to share. Reject manmade parenting treaties. Such will never stand the test of time. Challenge the children's best in the classroom, on the playground, and in the house of God. Only then will they understand their calling.

Above all, recognize that the only demands you need honor are to provide both love and limits. Even so, declining morals, dark statistics, and attacks on the sanctity of life will always be.

Fear not, God is with you. For as you love His children, so too, will He love you.

Found in Mir, Montana

Note From the Author

Dearest Reader,

Thank you for taking the time to read *Conquering the Culture: The Fight for Our Children's Souls*.

I trust there were times when you were angry, shocked, even disbelieving. And, though you may not have agreed with all Danika had to say, your motivation to listen was surely driven by your love and concern for children.

Whether parent, grandparent, or child advocate, you must continue your crusade to protect the gift of childhood. To help strengthen your resolve, may I offer nine parenting principles:

> I. PRAY that the Spirit of God will provide you with the wisdom to discern right from wrong, good from evil.
>
> II. FORGIVE those whose indifference and/or ignorance can lead to the destruction of family.
>
> III. Be PASSIONATE in your advocacy for truth, justice, and love.
>
> IV. Stay out of the DARC (avoiding Despair, Alienation, Radicalism and Cynicism).
>
> V. TRUST the soul to warn against impending darkness.
>
> VI. FOCUS on your "vision," ensuring compatibility with your spiritual journey.

VII. Be COURAGEOUS as you are challenged to defend your convictions and beliefs.

VIII. NETWORK with others whose compassion, resourcefulness and commitment to family, mirrors your own.

IX. Of your own FREE WILL, multiply in the lives of others, those talents received from God.

Though the journey will be long and hard, take comfort that raising children is not reserved for only the best of parents, but rather, for those parents (and grandparents) who can say they did their best.

DAVID PAUL EICH

Notes

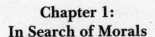

Chapter 1:
In Search of Morals

Part I: Wandering in the Moral Desert

Jan & Richard Letter—1 January

Frank S. Mead, *12,000 Religious Quotations* (Grand Rapids, Michigan: Baker House Books, 1989), 313.

Danika Letter—15 January

Richard Layman, *American Decades 1950-1959* (Detroit, MI: Gale Research Inc. 1994).

Ibid.

Roy Pickard, *The Oscar Movies: From A-Z* (Great Britain: Anchor Press Ltd., 1977).

"To Face the Wind" research project by Patti Theis (Akron, Ohio, January 1991).

Kids Count Data Book (Baltimore, MD: The Annie E. Casey Foundation, 1994), 15.

Part II: "What Is Truth?"

John & Ronica Letter—15 January

Robert Coles, "The Moral Life of the Young," Address to the American Society of Newspaper Editors (Cambridge, Massachusetts, 10 April 1991).

Danika Letter—18 January

William Bennett, *The Devaluing of America: The Fight for Our Culture and Our Children* (New York, NY: Summit Books, 1992), 60.

Part III—The Family ... New and Improved?

Herbert V. Prochnow and Herbert V. Prochnow, Jr., *5100 Quotations for Speakers and Writers* (Michigan: Baker Book House, 1992), 503.

Ralph L Woods, *The World Treasury of Religious Quotations* (New York: Hawthorn Books, Inc., 1966), 325.

Darcee Letter—5 February

"Speaking of Kids," A National Survey of Children and Parents, 1990 (National Commission On Children: 1991), 9.

Ibid.

Ibid.

Ibid.

National Commission on Children, "Beyond Rhetoric: A New American Agenda for Children and Families" (Library of Congress Cataloging-in-Publication Data, 1991), 27.

Darcee Letter—11 February

Richard Louv, *Childhood's Future* (San Diego, CA: Anchor Books, 1991), 19.

Danika Letter—11 February

Dr. James Dobson and Gary L. Bauer, *Children At Risk* (Dallas: Word Publishing 1990), 115.

Part IV—Professors and Prophets

Back to the Family Kaleidoscope (Akron, OH: In The Company Of Kids, December 1992), 1:3.

Danika Letter—14 February

Dr. Raymond Guarendi, *Back to the Family* (New York: Villard Books 1990), 61.

Ibid., 62.

Ibid., 61.

Chapter 2:
Rights—Responsibilities—Revolution

George Grant, *Trial And Error: The American Civil Liberties Union and Its Impact on Your Family* (Brentwood, TN: Wolgemuth & Hyatt Publishers, Inc., 1989), 98.

Part I—The Freedom Train

J.A. Smith and W.D Ross, "The Works of Aristotle" (Oxford: *Politica*, 1921), 10:1318.

Danika Letter—27 February

Luke 15:11-32

Jan & Richard Letter—2 March

"The Troubled Journey: A Profile of American Youth," report (Minneapolis, MN: The Search Institute).

Ibid.

Ibid.

Danika Letter—5 March

Ibid.

Ibid.

John Holt, *Escape from Childhood* (New York: Dutton, 1974), 158-59.

Darcee Letter—5 March

Ibid., 88.

Search Institute, "Troubled Journey" report.

Ibid.

Ibid.

Part II—Cornucopia Kids

Mark Masters and David Kupelian, "New Dimensions: The Psychology Behind the News" *The New Cold War* (June 1990): 50.

Danika Letter—14 March

Matthew 25:14-30

Part III—"Gonna Do It Anyway"

Carl F.H. Henry, "The Uneasy Conscience 45 Years Later: The Spiritual Predicament" as cited in *Vital Speeches of the Day* (Mount Pleasant, SC: 15 May 1992), 58:15.

Danika Letter—17 March

Claire Scovell, "Would You Believe It? Your Mom Was Wrong!" (Cosmopolitan, May 1992): 124, 126.

Information provided by Sue Alford, Advocates for Youth Researcher, 12 April 1995.

William A. Donohue, *The New Freedom: Individualism and Collectivism in the Social Lives of Americans* (New Brunswick, NJ: Transaction Publishers, 1990), 4.

Darcee Letter—17 March

Adolescent Services "Teen Talk Line," Total calls for 1990, Children's Hospital Medical Center of Akron.

Adelle Banks, "Some Kids Agree in Survey: Rape OK If Date Costs Money," *Los Angeles Herald Examiner* (8 May 1988), A:14.

Danika Letter—23 March

Dr. James Dobson and Gary L. Bauer, *Children At Risk* (Dallas: Word Publishing 1990), 221.

Darcee Letter—23 March

Dr. Raymond Guarendi, *Back to the Family* (New York: Villard Books 1990), 206.

Ibid.

Part IV—Victimology and Other Entitlements

William Raspberry, "What Manner of Man, Clarence Thomas?" (*Washington Post*, 3 July 1991), A:19.

Darcee Letter—25 March

Richard Louv, *Childhood's Future* (San Diego, CA: Anchor Books, 1991), 171.

Danika Letter—25 March

Charles J. Sykes, *A Nation of Victims: The Decay of the American Character* (New York: St. Martin's Press, 1992), 126.

Ibid., 148.

Chapter 3:
Hell's Heroes

Sen. Robert Byrd, Democrat, W. Virginia: "Speech on Senate Floor" (18 September 1991).

Part I—That's Entertainment

Michael Medved, *Hollywood vs. America: Popular Culture and the War on Traditional Values* (New York: HarperCollins Publishers, 1992), 279.

Jan & Richard Letter—18 April

Donald Wildmon, *The Home Invaders*, permission granted by Martha Swindle of the American Family Association (Tupelo, MS: 13 April 1995).

Ibid.

Darcee Letter—21 April

James F. Cooper, "New Dimensions: The Psychology Behind The News," *Art Censors: A Closer Look at the NEA* (June 1991), 28.

Part II—Reverse Role Models

Michael Medved, *Hollywood vs. America: Popular Culture And The War On Traditional Values* (New York: HarperCollins Publishers, 1992), 215.

Danika Letter—24 April

U.S. News & World Report (28 December 1992): 96.

Darcee Letter—24 April

1989 Lou Harris Poll

Danika Letter—30 April

Christopher Cerf & Victor Navasky, *The Experts Speak: The Definitive Compendium of Authoritative Misinformation* (New York, NY: Pantheon Books, 1984), 85.

Ibid., 129.

Darcee Letter—30 April

Howard E. Ferguson, *The Edge* (Cleveland, OH: Getting The Edge Company, 1983), 3:21.

Ibid., 1:4.

Ibid., 1:18.

Ibid., 2:8.

Ibid., 2:29.

Ibid., 7:25.

Part III—Freedom of Speech and Other Incantations

Carl F.H. Henry, "The Uneasy Conscience 45 Years Later: The Spiritual Predicament" as cited in *Vital Speeches Of The Day* (Mount Pleasant, SC: 15 May 1992), 58:15.

Darcee Letter—2 May

The National Coalition for the Protection of Children & Families, used with permission—Maryam Kubasek.

Part IV—Shock Theatre

Excerpt from the film *Fatal Addiction*. Copyright 1989, Focus on the Family. All rights reserved. International copyright secured. Used by permission.

Danika Letter—11 May

Cited to David per National Institute of Mental Health over the phone, June 1995.

Benjamin Alexander, "Is the Time for People of Good Will to Act—Over?"; Speech delivered at Bradley University, 30 October 1993.

Masters & Kupelian, "Sneak Attack On America's Culture", *New Dimensions* (June 1991): 21.

Ibid.

"Prime Time Viewing: Spring Sweeps, April 28—May 25, 1991" (Tupelo, MS: American Family Association, 1991).

Gallop Poll, 1991: (Cited in *Los Angeles Times*/Calendar, 3 November 1991), 81.

Danika Letter—May 17

From focus on the Family Newsletter. Copyright© 1994, focus on the family. All rights reserved. International copyright secured. Used by permission.

Permission granted by Barbara Wyatt, Parent's Music Resource Center, Arlington, VA.

Beverly LaHaye, *Who Will Save Our Children? 30 Strategies for Protecting Your Child from A Threatening World* (Brentwood, TN: Wolgemuth & Hyatt, Publishers, Inc. 1990), 157.

Chapter 4:
To Face the Wind

Part I—Dungeons, Dragons & Diversity

Frank S. Mead, *12,000 Religious Quotations* (Grand Rapids, MI: Baker House Books, 1989), 462.

Darcee Letter—22 June

Adelle Banks, "Some Kids Agree in Survey: Rape OK If Date Costs Money" *Los Angeles Herald Examiner*, 8 May 1988, A:14.

"Guidelines for Comprehensive Sexuality Education: Kindergarten Through Twelfth Grade" booklet (New York, NY: Sex Information and Education Council of the U.S., 1991), 11.

Ibid., 12.

Ibid., 15.

Ibid., 21.

Ibid., 26.

Ibid., 26.

Ibid., 28.

Ibid., 32.

Ibid., 33.

Ibid., 38.

Danika Letter—22 June

Focus On The Family, "In Defense of A Little Virginity," advertisement, 1994.

"Teenager's Bill of Rights" Teens Have the Right brochure, published by the Division of AIDS Program Services New York City Department of Health, January, 1991.

Danika Letter—28 June

SIECUS booklet, "Guidelines for Comprehensive Sexuality Education," 16.

Romans 1:26-27.

1 Timothy 1:9-10.

1 Corinthians 6:9.

Part II: Of Censorship and Sponsorship

Danika Letter—5 July

Morality In Media, Inc., used with permission from Bob Peters.

Ibid.

Ibid.

The National Coalition for the Protection of Children & Families, used with permission—Maryam Kubasek.

Ibid.

Darcee Letter—11 July

"Uniform Crime Reports" Table 38 (Washington, DC: FBI, 1993), 227.

Danika Letter—11 July

The American Heritage Dictionary of the English Language, 3d ed., s.v. "Complacency."

Ibid., 310.

Cal Thomas, "Censors Scream Loudest About Censorship," *Conservative Chronicle* (1 January 1992, vol. 7:1), 16.

Part III—Blacks and Whites and Shades of Gray

Mark 10:14.

Darcee Letter—17 July

Robert F. Drinan, *The Fractured Dream: America's Divisive Moral Choices* (New York: Crossroads, 1991), 45.

Danika Letter—17 July

"The Hippocratic Oath (circa 400 BC)," *The Catholic World* Report (April 1995): 50.

Darcee Letter—23 July

Christopher Cerf & Victor Navasky, *The Experts Speak: The Definitive Compendium of Authoritative Misinformation* (New York, NY: Pantheon Books, 1984), 34.

Danika Letter—23 July

William Burke, political philosopher, prediction reference.

Back to the Family Kaleidoscope (Akron, OH: In The Company Of Kids, November 1992), 1:3.

Part IV— In Search of Symbiosis

The New Millennium, Pat Robertson, 1990, Word, Inc., Dallas, Texas. All rights reserved.

Danika Letter—29 July

David Hocking, *The Moral Catastrophe: The future Survival of the American Family* (Harvest House Publisher, 1990), 26.

Eugene H. Methvin (*Reader's Digest*, November 1992), 75–77.

George R. Will, "Supreme Court Inciting Litigation" (*Conservative Chronicle*: 8 July 1992), 7:28, pp. 2.

Michael Medved, *Hollywood vs. America: Popular Culture and the War On Traditional Values* (New York: HarperCollins Publishers, 1992), 335.

Darcee Letter—4 August

Luke 20:25.

John 19:11.

Danika Letter—4 August

Robert F. Drinan, *The Fractured Dream: America's Divisive Moral Choices* (New York: Crossroads, 1991), 200.

William P. Barr, *The Judeo-Christian Tradition vs. Secularism,* Speech delivered at the Catholic League for Religious and Civil Rights (Washington, D.C., 6 October 1992).

Back to the Family Kaleidoscope (Akron, OH: In the Company of Kids, December 1992), 1:3.

Herbert V. Prochnow and Herbert V. Prochnow, Jr., *5100 Quotations for Speakers and Writers* (Michigan: Baker Book House, 1992), 421.

David Hocking, *The Moral Catastrophe: The Future Survival of the American Family* (Eugene, Oregon: Harvest House Publishers, 1990), 24.

Supreme Court Justice Earl Warren Breakfast in Washington (*Time Magazine*, 15 February 1954), 49.

II Timothy 3:1–4.

Chapter 5:
If I Only Had a Brain

Part I—To Reap What They Sow

Herbert V. Prochnow & Herbert V. Prochnow, Jr., *5100 Quotations for Speakers and Writers* (Grand Rapids, MI: Baker Book House, 1992), 380.

Danika Letter—16 August

Adele Jones, *NEA Today* (September 1994): 23.

Richard Louv, *Childhood's Future* (San Diego, CA: Anchor Books, 1991), 341.

Prochnow & Prochnow, Jr., *5100 Quotations,* 434.

Darcee Letter—22 August

Phyllis Schlafly, "OBE Conceals Gradual Lowering of Standards," *Conservative Chronicle* (22 December 1993), 11.

Danika Letter—22 August

"Harper's Index" (New York: Harper's Magazine, October 1990), 17.

George R. Will, "Educators Losing Battle to Mislead Public, *Conservative Chronicle* (22 September 1993), 17.

Part II—Back to the Catacombs

Darcee Letter—28 August

Louv, *Childhood's Future*, 338.

"Attacks On the Freedom to Learn," 15th annual survey (Washington, DC: People for the American Way, 1994).

Danika Letter—28 August

Beverly LaHaye, *Who Will Save Our Children? 30 Strategies for Protecting Your Child From a Threatening World* (Brentwood, TN: Wolgemuth & Hyatt Publishers, Inc., 1990), 104.

Jane Gross, "Where 'Boys Will Be Boys' and Adults Are Bewildered," *New York Times*, 29 March 1993, 1A.

William Bennett, *The Devaluing of America: The Fight for Our Culture and Our Children* (New York, NY: Summit Books, 1992), 35.

Proverbs 22:6.

Danika Letter—3 September

William Bennett, *The Devaluing of America: The Fight for Our Culture and Our Children* (New York, NY: Summit Books, 1992), 85.

Part III—Hi Ho, Hi Ho—It's Off to Welfare We Go

Permission granted by son, David Wessner, 12 April 1995.

Danika Letter—9 September

Roper Organization survey reported in *USA Today*, August 1991.

Charles W. Colson and Jack Eckerd, *Why America Doesn't Work*, 1991. Published by Word Publishers. Used by permission of Prison Fellowship Ministries, P.O. Box 17500, Washington, DC, 22041., 150.

Darcee Letter—15 September

Daniel Smith-Rowsey, "The Terrible Twenties," *Newsweek* (1 July 1991).

Danika Letter—15 September

"Values and Behavior Survey," used with permission by Jozelle Smith (Marina Del Rey, CA: Josephson Institute of Ethics, 1993).

Louv, *Childhood's Future*, 59.

Ibid., 86.

Colson and Eckerd, *Why America Doesn't Work*, 60.

Part IV—Condoms, Cucumbers & Counseling

Louv, *Childhood's Future*, 150.

Darcee Letter—21 September

Floyd G. Brown, "Life and Death In Arkansas," *National Review* (26 April 1993): 38–39.

Laurence Steinberg, Ph.D. and Ann Levine, *You & Your Adolescent: A Parent's Guide for Ages 10-20* (New York, NY: Harper & Row, 1990), 136.

"Guidelines for Comprehensive Sexuality Education: Kindergarten Through Twelfth Grade" (New York, NY: Sex Information and Education Council of the US, 1991), 11.

Ibid.

Danika Letter—21 September

Centers for Disease Control Division of STD/HIV Prevention, Annual Report 1993.

M. Howard & J. B. McCabe, Helping Teenagers Postpone Sexual Involvement (Family Planning Perspectives 1990), 22:1.

"Guidelines for Comprehensive Sexuality Education," SIECUS, 3.

Ibid.

"The Sex Education Manual," (Atlanta, GA: Georgia Department of Education, 1993).

Theresa Crenshaw, Speaker, "National Conference on HIV" (Washington, D.C., 15–18 November 1991).

Lynn Stanley, *Combat Ready: How to Fight the Culture War* (Lafayette, LA: Huntington House Publishers, 1995), 116.

Danika Letter—27 September

David Van Biema, "For the Love of Kids," *Time* (1 November 1993), 51.

Part V—Forbidden Fruit

John Bartlett, *Bartlett's Familiar Quotations* (Boston, MA: Little, Brown & Company), 283.

Danika Letter—3 October

Robert Leitman, *The Metropolitan Life survey of the American Teacher 1993: Violence In America's Public Schools* (New York, NY: Louis Harris and Associates, Inc., 1993), 7.

Beverly LaHaye, *Who Will Save Our Children? 30 Strategies for Protecting Your Child From A Threatening World* (Brentwood, TN: Wolgemuth & Hyatt, Publishers, Inc. 1990), 102.

Darcee Letter—8 October

Convention on the Rights of the Child, Articles from the United Nations General Assembly's Forty Fourth Session (Agenda Item 108, 5 December 1989).

U.S. Constitution Article VI, Paragraph 2.

Danika Letter—8 October

United Nation's General Assembly. Forty-fourth session, Convention on the Rights of the Child. A/108. 5 December 1989.

Darcee Letter—11 October

Used with permission per David Heffernon (Washington, DC: Children's Defense Fund, 11 April 1995).

Danika Letter—12 October

Raymond Guarendi, Ph.D., *Back to the Family* (New York, NY: Villard Books, 1991), Jacket cover.

We welcome comments from our readers. Feel free to write to us at the following address:

Editorial Department
Huntington House Publishers
P.O. Box 53788
Lafayette, LA 70505

More Good Books from Huntington House

Combat Ready
How to Fight the Culture War
by Lynn Stanley

The culture war between traditional values and secular humanism is escalating. At stake are our children. The schools, the liberal media, and even the government, through Outcome Based Education, are indoctrinating our children with moral relativism, instead of moral principles. *Combat Ready* not only discloses the extent to which our society has been influenced by this "anything goes" mentality. It offers sound advice about how parents can protect their children and restore our culture to its biblical foundation.

ISBN 1-56384-074-X

Handouts and Pickpockets:
Our Government Gone Berserk
by William P. Hoar

In his new book, William P. Hoar, a noted political analyst, echoes the sentiments of millions of Americans who are tired of being victimized by their own government. Hoar documents attacks on tradition in areas as diverse as the family and the military and exposes wasteful and oppressive tax programs. This chronicle of our government's pitiful decline into an overgrown Nanny State is shocking, but more shocking is Hoar's finding that this degeneration was no accident.

ISBN 1-56384-102-9

Can Families Survive in Pagan America?
by Samuel Dresner

Drug addiction, child abuse, divorce, and the welfare state have dealt terrible, pounding blows to the family structure. At the same time, robbery, homicide, and violent assaults have increased at terrifying rates. But, according to the author, we can restore order to our country and our lives. Using the tenets of Jewish family life and faith, Dr. Dresner calls on Americans from every religion and walk of life to band together and make strong, traditional families a personal and national priority again—before it's too late.

ISBN Trade Paper: 1-56384-080-4

Global Bondage— The U.N. Plan to Rule the World
by Cliff Kincaid

The U.N. is now openly laying plans for a World Government—to go along with its already functioning World Army. These plans include global taxation and an International Criminal Court that could prosecute American citizens. In *Global Bondage,* journalist Cliff Kincaid blows the lid off the United Nations. He warns that the move toward global government is gaining ground and that it will succeed if steps are not taken to stop it.

ISBN: 1-56384-103-7 Tradepaper
ISBN: 1-56384-109-6 Hardcover

The Best of HUMAN EVENTS Fifty Years of Conservative Thought and Action
Edited by James C. Roberts

Before Ronald Reagan, before Barry Goldwater, since the closing days of World War II, HUMAN EVENTS stood against the prevailing winds of the liberal political Zeitgeist. HUMAN EVENTS has published the best of three generations of conservative writers—academics, journalists, philosophers, politicians: Frank Chodorov and Richard Weaver, Henry Hazlitt and Hans Sennholz, William F. Buckley and M. Stanton Evans, Jack Kemp and Dan Quayle. A representative sample of their work, marking fifty years of American political and social history, is here collected in a single volume.

ISBN 1-56384-018-9

Political Correctness:
The Cloning of the American Mind
by David Thibodaux, Ph.D

The author, a professor of literature at the University of Southwestern Louisiana, confronts head on the movement that is now being called Polictical Correctness. Political correctness, says Thibodaux, "is an umbrellas under which advocates of civil rights, gay and lesbian rights, feminism, and environmental causes have gathered." To incur the wrath of these groups, one only has to disagree with them on political, moral, or social issues. To express traditionally Western concepts in universities today can result in not only ostracism, but even suspension. (According to a recent "McNeil-Lehrer News Hour" report, one student was suspended for discussing the reality of the moral law with an avowed homosexual. He was reinstated only after he apologized.)

ISBN: 1-56384-026-X

Beyond Political Correctness:
Are There Limits to This Lunacy?
by David Thibodaux, Ph.D

Author of the best-selling *Political Correctness: The Cloning of the American Mind*, Dr. David Thibodaux now presents his long awaited sequel—*Beyond Political Correctness: Are There Limits to This Lunacy?* The politically correct movement has now moved beyond college campuses. The movement has succeeded in turning the educational system of this country into a system of indoctrination. Its effect on education was predictable: steadily declining scores on every conceivable test which measures student performance; and, increasing numbers of college freshmen who know a great deal about condoms, homosexuality, and abortion, but who basic skills in language, math, and science are alarmingly deficient.

ISBN: 1-56384-066-9

Anyone Can Homeschool
How to Find What Works for You
by Terry Dorian, Ph.D., and Zan Peters Tyler

Honest, practical, and inspirational, *Anyone Can Homeschool* assesses the latest in homeschool curricula and confirms there are social as well as academic advantages to home education. Both veteran and novice homeschoolers will gain insight and up-to-date information from this important new book.

ISBN Trade Paper: 1-56384-095-2

Out of Control—
Who's Watching Our Child
Protection Agencies?
by Brenda Scott

This book of horror stories is true. The deplorable and unauthorized might of Child Protection Services is capable of reaching into and destroying any home in America. No matter how innocent and happy your family may be, you are one accusation away from disaster. Social workers are allowed to violate constitutional rights and often become judge, jury, and executioner. Innocent parents may appear on computer registers and be branded "child abuser" for life. Every year, it is estimated that over 1 million people are falsely accused of child abuse in this country. You could be next, says author and speaker Brenda Scott.

ISBN 1-56384-069-3

One Man, One Woman, One Lifetime
An Argument for Moral Tradition
by Reuven Bulka

Lifestyles that have been recognized since antiquity as destructive and immoral are promoted today as acceptable choices. Rabbi Reuven Bulka challenges the notion that contemporary society has outgrown the need for moral guidelines. Using both scientific research and classical biblical precepts, he examines changing sexual mores and debunks the arguments offered by activists and the liberal media.

ISBN 1-56384-079-0

Getting Out:
An Escape Manual for Abused Women
by Kathy L. Cawthon

Four million women are physically assaulted by their husbands, ex-husbands, and boyfriends each year. Of these millions of women, nearly 4,000 die. Kathy Cawthon, herself a former victim of abuse, uses her own experience and the expertise of law enforcement personnel to guide the reader through the process of escaping an abusive relationship. *Getting Out* also shows readers how they can become whole and healthy individuals instead of victims, giving them hope for a better life in the future.

ISBN: 1-56384-093-6

Children No More:
How We Lost a Generation
by Brenda Scott

Child abuse, school yard crime, gangland murders, popular lyrics laced with death motifs, twisted couplings posing as love on MTV and daytime soap operas (both accessible by latch-key children), loving parents portrayed as the enemy, condom pushers, drug apologists, philandering leaders . . . is it any wonder heroes and role models are passe? The author grieves the loss of a generation but savors a hope that the next can be saved.

ISBN 1-56384-083-9

Can Families Survive in
Pagan America?
by Samuel Dresner

Drug addiction, child abuse, divorce, and the welfare state have dealt terrible, pounding blows to the family structure. At the same time, robbery, homicide, and violent assaults have increased at terrifying rates. But, according to the author, we can restore order to our country and our lives. Using the tenets of Jewish family life and faith, Dr. Dresner calls on Americans from every religion and walk of life to band together and make strong, traditional families a personal and national priority again—before it's too late.

ISBN Trade Paper: 1-56384-080-4